MEDIA
LITERACY
THINKING CRITICALLY ABOUT
ADVERTISING

Peyton Paxson

WALCH EDUCATION®

SGS-SFI/COC-US09/5501

1   2   3   4   5   6   7   8   9   10

ISBN 978-0-8251-6512-2

Copyright © 2002, 2009
J. Weston Walch, Publisher
40 Walch Drive • Portland, ME 04103
www.walch.com

Printed in the United States of America

Contents

Contents

Contents

Unit 7: Advertising and the New Media

To the Teacher

THE MAGAZINE PUBLISHERS OF AMERICA tell us:

Today's teenagers reflect a diverse and complicated cross-section of attitudes, ethnicities, and perspectives. They are being bombarded by more information from more media sources than any group of teens in history. Because they've been exposed to constant advertising their entire lives, today's teens readily form brand opinions that will continue to influence their purchase decisions into their adult years.

Besides representing a new baby boom, today's teenagers have an income that enables discretionary spending. But that's not all. According to *Teen People*, teenagers' influence on purchases made by other people—such as parents and grandparents—represents an even larger amount of spending than their own.

Teenagers—the so-called Millennial Generation or Generation Y—use more media than previous generations, and they also use different media. Many advertisers have shifted their focus away from print media and television as they strive to reach teenagers. Today, advertisers seek out teenaged customers through social networking Web sites, within video games, via text messaging, and through blogs. The interactivity of new media allows advertisers to gather personal information about the teenagers who use those media and direct increasingly customized messages to them.

This revised book, part of a series on media literacy, focuses on advertising. Young people usually acknowledge the pervasiveness of advertising, but tend to deny that advertising affects them. Teenagers are especially attractive to advertisers because teenagers spend most of their income on heavily advertised consumer products and services; because they strongly influence purchasing decisions by older adults; and because teenagers are beginning to develop lifetime habits and brand loyalties. Thus, teenagers are carefully studied by the advertising industry; teenagers must respond in kind.

The guiding principle of this book is that the study of advertising can be used to teach critical-thinking skills. The units in this book provide students with information about advertising as a marketing medium, as a source of information, and as a source of social and cultural exchange.

The activities require students to describe this new information and apply it in varied exercises. Students will analyze and evaluate advertising techniques and the effect advertising has on how we identify ourselves. Ultimately, this book strives to make students more informed and more discerning consumers of advertising.

ADVERTISERS WANT YOUR ATTENTION! The reason is simple—advertisers want your money. The Newspaper Association of America estimates that Americans between the ages of 12 and 17 spent nearly $179 billion in 2006. Overall, teenagers in the United States spend an average of about $107 each week.

You are also seen by advertisers as being strongly brand-loyal. This means that you are willing to pay more for certain brands that are popular with you and your friends. Advertising research also indicates that teenagers develop purchasing habits that may continue for many years, perhaps for the rest of your life. You might feel that you personally are immune to the power of advertising, and that you are wise to what advertisers are up to. If so, look around your home, and count how many heavily advertised products you find.

The purpose of each activity is to:

- present you with methods for evaluating the quality of the information that advertising provides

- encourage you to investigate the effect advertising has on consumers

- help you become more knowledgeable about how advertisers get your attention, what messages they want you to receive, and sometimes, what advertisers don't want you to know about advertising

The objectives of this unit are to help students:

- understand the relationship between mass production, mass marketing, and mass media

- recognize that advertising evolves as society changes

- assess the economic consequences of advertising

- understand the basic structure of the advertising industry today

In This Unit

The Evolution of Advertising asks students to discuss changes in advertising with older adults.

The Best Class Activity in the Entire World! helps students recognize empty promises and specious comparisons.

The U.S Government and Advertising has students assess the use of advertising by the federal government.

Reach and Frequency requires students to distinguish between different types of consumer products and the different methods of advertising used to sell them.

Brand Loyalty and Consumer Involvement helps students understand the role that advertising plays in creating consumer perceptions about goods in the marketplace.

Prescription Drugs and Advertising allows students to evaluate the consequences that the heavy advertising of products has on consumer prices.

Commercial Speech introduces students to the tension between a business's freedom of speech and social concerns about advertising.

Advertising and Pseudo-Events introduces students to one form of stealth marketing frequently used by advertisers.

OCCASIONALLY, WE SEE advertisements that promote a category of product rather than a specific brand. For example, the "Got Milk?" advertisements are paid for by many milk companies and do not advertise a particular brand of milk. These types of advertisements are rare, however. Most advertisements are for particular brands of products. Branding, as identified by a name (such as Pepsi) or a **logo** (a symbol, such as the Nike swoosh), has been around for many years. However, branding did not become common until the late 1800s. Before that time, products were often sold generically, which means without a brand. A shopper in the mid-1800s would go to the store and simply ask for sugar, instead of asking for a particular brand of sugar.

The industrial revolution of the 1800s brought mass manufacturing of both products and packaging. New machines allowed companies to make hundreds of items in the same time it took to make a single item only a few years before. Since manufacturers could now mass-produce products, there was a need to mass-market those products.

The marketing business has four primary concerns, usually called the Four *P*'s: product, price, place, and promotion.

Product is the item sold, whether a tangible good (for example, a candy bar) or an intangible service (having your clothes cleaned by a dry cleaner). Today most goods are sold in packages. The package is practical (it holds the product), and it also identifies the brand of that product. Just as mass manufacturing allows for the faster and cheaper manufacturing of products, it also allows for the faster and cheaper manufacturing of boxes, bags, cans, and bottles to contain those products.

Price means the cost of the product—if the maker of a product charges too little, it will lose money on each product sold. Too low a price also might scare away some consumers, who believe the product must be of very poor quality if sold at too low a price. If the maker of a product charges too much, it will drive away people who might otherwise buy the product. In the late 1800s, as new machines made it easier to make products, the products became cheaper to make as the speed of machines made the manufacturing process more efficient. The products could be sold at lower prices. As a result, many manufacturers were able to sell products as different as sewing machines and shoes to people who either had not been able to afford them before, or who had not bought them as frequently as they now could.

Place includes distributing the product— getting the product from the manufacturer to the consumer. Distribution improved greatly in the late 1800s, as American railroads rapidly expanded. This allowed a manufacturer of a product on the West Coast of the United States to sell its products on the East Coast, and vice versa. For the first time, a manufacturer could have a truly national market for its products. (Some food products, such as iceberg lettuce, were specifically developed so that they could be transported by rail across the country without spoiling.) Today, place includes such issues as making certain that a consumer can obtain a product quickly and conveniently. The Internet has greatly expanded advertisers' sense of place, as one can shop online with sellers all over the world.

Promotion focuses on advertising, the subject of this book. In order to create a mass market for their mass-produced products, manufacturers began to advertise in magazines and newspapers, creating the first mass media. Mass media (*media* is the plural of *medium*) are designed to get a lot of information transmitted to a lot of people, usually as quickly as possible. Just as mechanization had made it easier and cheaper to make products and their packaging, improvements in printing technology made it easier to print relatively inexpensive newspapers and magazines, which rely on advertisements to make a profit.

Early advertisements were relatively simple and did little "selling." Many of these advertisements were called tombstones, because they were nothing more than a few words on a rectangle or a square, just like a grave marker in a cemetery. They often just told consumers that a product existed and asked consumers to buy it. For example, a newspaper advertisement from the 1890s might simply say, "Please try Jones's Biscuits." In the early 1900s, advertisers realized that they had to compete more aggressively against each other, and instead of creating their own advertising, many advertisers began to seek help of advertising agencies.

Today, most of the advertisements you see are created by advertising agencies. These firms are composed of specialized professionals; some agencies have hundreds of employees. Advertising agency personnel include copywriters, who write the words that are read in a print advertisement or spoken in a radio or television advertisement. Commercial artists design the "look" of advertisements, choose the type of lettering that is used, the colors used, and so forth.

Advertising researchers try to determine what types of messages and images are most effective in selling the different types of products advertised. Advertising buyers decide which publications and broadcast media to advertise in, and negotiate prices for that advertising.

Professional advertising agencies do not merely announce that a product is for sale; they try to give us a "reason why" we should buy the advertised product. Some of these reasons why seem obvious, such as when a laundry detergent is advertised as getting your clothes clean. Some of these reasons why seem more subtle. For example, look at an advertisement for a soft drink like Pepsi or Sprite, and try to determine what reason the advertisement gives you for buying the product.

Through the early part of the last century, advertising usually took the form of words on paper, whether in a magazine, a newspaper, a mailing, or a point-of-purchase display. In the 1920s, commercial radio became available as a new advertising medium, and television followed 20 years later. It was not until the 1990s that the next important advertising medium arose—the Internet. These different types of media are discussed in different sections of this book.

It is important to note that each of these media—magazines, newspapers, radio, television, and the Internet—rely heavily on advertisers to make money. The consumer only partially pays for the cost of providing these media.

The media charge advertisers for advertising based on space or time. This means that print and Internet advertising prices are based on how large the advertisement is; television and radio advertising prices are based on how long the advertisement is. The price of advertising is also based on how many people will see the advertisement. For example, a one-page advertisement in a newspaper that 1,000 people read will usually be much less expensive than the same-sized advertisement in a newspaper read by millions of people. A 30-second advertisement that plays on a television channel at 3 A.M. (when most of us are sleeping) will be much less expensive than a 30-second advertisement shown during a popular program at 8 P.M. Independent organizations measure the number of readers of print media (called readership), the number of listeners of radio (listenership), or number of viewers of television (viewership) in order to provide reliable information to advertisers. This way, advertisers know how many people they're paying to reach.

Advertising changes as the media change. Teenagers watch less television than most other age groups do. Advertisers know this, and today they pursue the teen market through advertisements that appear on online social networking sites such as MySpace and Facebook, in video games, and in text messaging.

With the increase in the number of advertisers and advertising media over time, it has become harder and harder for individual advertisers to break through the clutter and get (and keep) our attention. As a result, advertisers are constantly looking for and experimenting with new ways to get us to buy their products. One thing has not changed—advertisers still try to make us think we need or want whatever it is they are trying to sell.

This 1923 advertisement for the Jordan Playboy automobile appealed to a desire among some car buyers for adventure rather than mere transportation. Although this advertisement was ahead of its time, its approach is common in automobile advertising today.

The Evolution of Advertising -

ADVERTISING BECAME a standard part of the business world more than 150 years ago. Since then, American society has changed. Most people lived on farms 150 years ago; now, most Americans live in cities. After World War II ended in 1945, more Americans started going to college than before. Technology has changed, bringing new advertising media, including television and the Internet. Technology has also brought more things to advertise, such as computers and cell phones. Just as society continues to change, so does advertising.

Consider the following questions. Write your response in the space provided. Use another sheet of paper, if necessary.

Interview an adult who is 40 years old or older to learn how advertising has changed over the years.

1. How has the pacing of television advertising changed? Do advertisements today seem to have a quicker pace or a slower pace than they used to?

2. What do you think are some of the reasons for these changes?

3. How has the music used in television advertising changed?

4. What do you think are some of the reasons for these changes?

5. How have magazine advertisements changed?

6. What do you think are some of the reasons for these changes?

7. How has technology changed how you view advertising? Explain.

The Best Class Activity in the Entire World!-------

MANY ADVERTISEMENTS rely on what is known as **puffery,** making a claim that sounds good, but cannot really be evaluated. For example, if an automobile manufacturer tells you that its new car is "the hottest buy in America," how does one evaluate or measure that claim? If a product is advertised as "America's favorite," what does that really mean?

Many advertisements use comparative adjectives (usually, words ending in –er, such as better, faster, stronger) or superlative words (usually words ending in –est, such as best, smartest, cleanest). But such words only mean something when one knows how to make the comparison. For example, if you are told that one package of gum is larger than another package, you can compare the weight of each package, or the number of pieces of gum. But how does one compare which gum is "fresher" than another?

Write your response in the space provided. Use another sheet of paper, if necessary.

1. Why do you think advertisers use puffery so often?

2. Look through some newspapers and magazines and find advertisements for three different goods or services that use puffery to try to sell a product. Attach the advertisements to this page. On the next page, fill in the chart with each advertised product, an example of puffery found in the ad, and an explanation as to why the example can be considered puffery.

Activity 2: The Best Class Activity in the Entire World! *(continued)*

Product	Example of puffery	Why is this puffery?
Snapple	"Made from the Best Stuff on Earth"	The word *best* is a matter of personal opinion that cannot be measured. The word *stuff* is vague.

The U.S. Government and Advertising - - - - - - - - - - -

THE FEDERAL GOVERNMENT of the United States raises most of the money it needs to operate by taxing the income of people who live and work in the United States, and taxing corporations that do business in the United States. Many American taxpayers fall within a 28 percent tax bracket for most income. This means the taxpayer must give 28 percent of the taxable income she or he earns each year to the federal government. The government uses this money for hundreds of different purposes, including paying for the military, providing financial help to unemployed people, and helping state and local governments build roads and airports.

The U.S government also spends money on advertising. In 2006, for example, the U.S. government was the 29th largest advertiser in the country, just behind top national retailer Target, and many millions of dollars ahead of Home Depot and Wal-Mart. The U.S. government spent nearly $1.133 billion on advertising that year. This included nearly $400 million on television advertising and more than $40 million on Internet advertising.

Consider the following questions. Write your response in the space provided. Use another sheet of paper, if necessary.

1. According to the United States Census Bureau, there are about 304 million Americans. How much does the federal government spend on total advertising per American?

2. In your opinion, do you think that it is a good idea or a bad idea that our government spends so much of our money on advertising? Why? Explain.

3. Consider the opinion opposite of yours. If you approve of the government spending taxpayer money on advertising, write the best argument against that spending. If you are against government spending on advertising, write what you think is the best argument in favor of that spending.

Most of the U.S. government's spending on advertising focuses on recruiting for the military. However, the federal government also spends many millions of dollars to tell the public about other governmental activities or to discuss social concerns.

4. Besides the military, list two other governmental activities or social concerns that you think it would be important for the federal government to advertise. Explain why you think each is important.

Reach and Frequency -

WHEN ADVERTISERS decide how much money they want to spend to advertise a particular product, they have to decide on matters of **reach** and **frequency.** Reach is concerned with how many people see an advertisement, and in how large a geographical area. For example, the owner of a local bakery would not want to spend the money it would cost to advertise that bakery all across the country or across the state. Because the bakery might only expect to sell its products to people in the community where it is located, it would only want to pay to advertise to the people who would actually shop at that bakery. On the other hand, Wrigley advertises its chewing gum throughout the country, because many Americans chew gum, and because Wrigley products are available everywhere in the country.

Frequency is a way of describing how many advertisements an advertiser uses, and how often. Frequency can be measured in a single medium (such as newspapers) or in a variety of media (newspapers, radio, television, magazines, billboards, etc.). Products that tend to have little brand loyalty and are purchased (or repurchased) often will usually have frequent advertisements. For example, advertising for shampoos and fast-food restaurants often stresses frequency.

Consider the following questions. Write your response in the space provided. Use another sheet of paper, if necessary.

1. Complete the chart below. Name three types of products that you think should emphasize reach of advertising, trying to reach as much of the American population as possible. Explain why you think advertising for this type of product would emphasize reach.

Type of product	Why reach?

Activity 4: Reach and Frequency *(continued)*

2. Complete the chart below. List three types of products that you think should emphasize frequency of advertising, trying to run as many advertisements as often as possible. Explain why you think advertising for this type of product would emphasize frequency.

Type of product	Why frequency?

Brand Loyalty and Consumer Involvement --------

BRAND LOYALTY, or the lack of brand loyalty, is an important concern for advertisers. Brand loyalty means that many people who use a product have a favorite brand, may go to a little extra trouble to find it, and might even be willing to pay more for it than other brands.

Some advertisers have developed brand loyalty for their product by spending millions and millions of dollars on advertising, which keeps the product's name in consumers' minds. Other companies have developed brand loyalty mostly through word of mouth: people tried the product or service, liked it, and recommended it to their friends. Many products and services have developed brand loyalty through a combination of these processes.

Consider the following questions. Write your response in the space provided. Use another sheet of paper, if necessary.

1. List three brands of products or services that you or people you know are very loyal to.

   a.

   b.

   c.

2. List three reasons why people might be loyal to a particular brand.

   a.

   b.

   c.

3. One of the products or services that people feel very little brand loyalty to is their cell phone service provider. This is why cell phone service providers spend so much money on advertising.

   Why do you think that many cell phone users are not loyal to their cell phone service provider?

4. List three types of products or services (other than cell phone service providers) that you or people you know have very *little* brand loyalty to.

   a.

   b.

   c.

5. List three reasons why people might not care which brand of product they buy.

   a.

   b.

   c.

"Consumer involvement" is a marketing concept that examines how much time people think about a product before they purchase it. For example, since a car is a very expensive investment, the decision to buy a car has high consumer involvement. Many car buyers do research in magazines and on the Internet before buying a car, and may investigate several different cars before making a decision. Low consumer involvement would be associated with "impulse" purchases, or routine purchases. For example, a person might buy whichever brand of paper towel is the cheapest at the store that day, or buy the brand that has the biggest display in the store. Low-involvement purchases are often heavily influenced by **point-of-purchase advertising.**

Whether a product is a high-involvement or low-involvement item should not be confused with brand loyalty. For example, some people will buy a particular brand of paper towels because that is the brand they always buy (without really thinking about why), and some people buy whatever brand is cheapest, or whichever brand they see first.

6. In this chart, list three types of products that you would consider high-involvement items. Explain why each is a high-involvement item.

Type of product	Why high involvement?

7. What sorts of messages do you think that advertisers for high-involvement items should give in their advertisements?

8. In this chart, list three types of products that you would consider to be low-involvement items. Explain why each is a low-involvement item.

Type of product	Why low involvement?

9. What sorts of messages do you think that advertisers for low-involvement items should give in their advertisements?

Prescription Drugs and Advertising - - - - - - - - - - - -

THERE ARE TWO BASIC FORMS of medical drugs. Prescription drugs require a note from a doctor in order to buy that drug from a pharmacy. Over-the-counter drugs can be purchased without a prescription at a pharmacy, grocery store, and so forth. Drugs that require a prescription are considered to be particularly dangerous if misused. To prevent misuse, the federal government requires the advice of a doctor before a person can buy prescription drugs.

For many years, companies that make prescription drugs were not allowed to advertise those drugs on television without giving many warnings about problems that might occur when taking those drugs. The warnings were usually so long that it cost too much money for prescription drug makers to advertise on television. Those drug companies relied instead on magazine and newspaper advertisements.

Drug companies also relied heavily on salespeople who would visit doctors. You may have noticed how much advertising your own doctor has in his or her office for different drugs, on things such as coffee cups and notepads. This type of advertising is called **push marketing.** Push/pull marketing refers to the customer's purchasing experience. In push marketing, advertisers "push" what they want to sell toward customers through a variety of methods.

In 1997, the U.S. Food and Drug Administration (FDA) changed its rule and said that prescription drugs could be advertised on television, as long as the advertisements told of ways that people could get more information about those drugs. Other sources of information include a Web site or a toll-free telephone number. This type of advertising, called direct-to-consumer advertising, is a type of **pull marketing.** In pull marketing, customers "pull" information about what they want to buy toward themselves.

Consider the following questions. Write your response in the space provided. Use another sheet of paper, if necessary.

1. Name a product that is advertised using push marketing. Look at some ads on television or in magazines and newspapers to identify one. Why do you think this product is advertised using push marketing? Explain.

2. Name a product that is advertised using pull marketing. (*Hint:* Think about things sold in the grocery store.) Why do you think this product is advertised using pull marketing? Explain.

Since the FDA's rule changed in 1997, consumers have seen many advertisements for prescription drugs on television, in magazines and newspapers, and on the Internet. Today, six of the largest U.S. advertisers are companies that manufacture prescription drugs. The amount of money people spend on prescription drugs has increased significantly.

3. Why do you think many of the most popular prescription drugs today are also the most heavily advertised? Explain.

4. When you buy a product that is heavily advertised, who really is paying for the advertising of that product? Explain.

Some people think it was a good idea when the FDA changed its regulations and allowed prescription drug makers to advertise more easily on television. Some people think it was a bad idea.

5. Describe one reason why direct-to-consumer drug advertising might be a good idea.

6. Describe one reason why direct-to-consumer drug advertising might be a bad idea.

7. Overall, do you think direct-to-consumer drug advertising is a good idea or bad idea? Explain.

Commercial Speech ------------------------------

PRIVATE CITIZENS ENJOY freedom of speech and are protected by the First Amendment of the U.S. Constitution. However, the courts have decided that although corporations and other businesses have some First Amendment protection, commercial speech (including advertising) is not as protected as personal speech.

Consider the following questions. Write your response in the space provided. Use another sheet of paper, if necessary.

1. Why do you think the courts say that there is a higher degree of freedom for personal speech than there is for advertising? Explain.

For many years, states prohibited the advertising of prices for prescription drugs. In 1976, the U.S. Supreme Court said this was a violation of pharmacists' First Amendment right to free speech. However, very few pharmacies discuss their prices in their advertising today.

2. Why do you think that most pharmacies do not choose to advertise their prices? Explain.

3. Do you think that it is a good thing for consumers that pharmacies do not advertise their prices? Explain.

In the past, many states forbade lawyers from advertising at all. In 1977, the U.S. Supreme Court said that this was a violation of lawyers' First Amendment rights.

4. Do you think that advertising by lawyers is good for society or not? Explain.

Legal organizations and advertising firms have studied lawyers' advertising. They found that people think that lawyers who advertise in the phone book are more reliable than lawyers who advertise on television.

5. Explain why you think that people find lawyers who advertise in the phone book are more reliable than lawyers who advertise on television.

Advertising and Pseudo-Events - - - - - - - - - - - - - - - -

THE PREFIX *PSEUDO* means "fake" (for example, you may know hip-hop artist and producer Timothy Z. Mosley by his **pseudonym,** or fake name, Timbaland). Advertisers often try to create **pseudo-events,** or fake news events, that focus on their product. For example, the Super Bowl game each year, which many sports fans consider a "real" event, includes the first showing of expensively made advertisements that often feature major celebrities and special effects. These advertisements usually receive lots of attention from the news media before and after they are shown for the first time. These advertisements are pseudo-events when they are treated as "news."

Another example of a pseudo-event occurred when the makers of M&M's candy asked consumers to vote on what color to change the light brown shade of its candy to—the choices were purple and blue. Blue was the winner, and the makers of M&M's paid to have New York City's Empire State Building lit up in blue at night to "celebrate" the winner. This pseudo-event received major coverage in the news media, including television and newspapers. Generating hype around pseudo-events is one form of **stealth marketing.** Stealth marketing occurs when an advertiser engages in marketing activities but tries to make it look as if it is not.

Consider the following questions. Write your response in the space provided. Use another sheet of paper, if necessary.

1. Find examples of a pseudo-event by paying careful attention to television programs or newspaper and magazine articles for a week or so. What examples did you find? List all the examples you found.

2. Choose one of the examples. Explain why the example you chose is a pseudo-event.

3. Review the Ad Buzz for this unit. Why do you think the media often willingly cooperate with advertisers who try to create these fake events?

The objectives of this unit are to help students:

- recognize the pervasiveness of advertising in American society

- understand why advertisers are strongly attracted to consumers in certain age groups and less attracted to consumers in other age groups

- examine puffery and other empty claims made in advertising

- explore the use of celebrity endorsements in advertising

In This Unit

Tobacco Advertising and Teenagers has students confront past efforts of major tobacco companies to market cigarettes to teenagers.

Advertising at School helps students understand the pervasiveness of advertising in American society.

Advertising and Problems: "Let the Product Be the Hero" introduces students to a standard advertising technique—highlighting a problem and offering the product as the solution.

What Is the Advertisement Really Saying? provides students with a chance to learn how different products are targeted to different consumers.

Advertising and Age has students consider advertisers' levels of interest in older versus younger audiences and then discuss advertising issues with senior citizens.

Advertising and Ethnicity encourages students to consider the role of ethnicity in advertising.

Celebrities and Advertising allows students to explore the role that athletes and entertainers play in advertising.

Advertising and the Hierarchy of Needs has students apply the different stages of Maslow's Hierarchy of Needs to the marketing of consumer goods.

Army Advertising further explores Maslow's Hierarchy of Needs, asking students to examine the Army's three most recent advertising campaigns.

THE AVERAGE AMERICAN sees about 3,000 advertisements per day. By high school graduation, you will have watched about 350,000 television commercials. This may sound like too high a figure, but consider the fact that U.S. businesses spend more than $285 billion on advertising each year. That is nearly $1,000 spent for every man, woman, and child in the country. Whether it is effective or not, a lot of money is being spent on advertising.

What is an advertisement? Sometimes, advertisements are obvious—a 30-second commercial on television, a full-page advertisement in a magazine, or a billboard on the side of a highway. Sometimes, advertisements are more subtle. This can include types of **stealth marketing**—sneaky marketing that does not look like advertising, but is. Just a few examples:

- Advertisers pay movie and television producers to show their product being used by the characters in a movie or television show; this practice is called **product placement.**

- Videos on MTV and other music-oriented channels are basically advertisements for recording companies.

- Fashion magazines such as *Seventeen* contain articles about celebrities that tell the reader what brands of cosmetics those celebrities wear; the cosmetic companies pay to have that information published.

- *The Price Is Right* and other television game shows feature dozens of name-brand products on every program.

- Corporations sponsor events, such as football games (The FedEx Orange Bowl)

or Beyonce's concert tour sponsored by Pepsi. Even Pope John Paul II's visit to Mexico in 1999 was sponsored by Frito-Lay and Pepsi!

Advertisers divide consumers into categories called **demographics** and **psychographics.** Demographics are statistics about people grouped by such information as age, gender, ethnicity, geography, and income. Psychographics are statistics about people grouped by their interests, attitudes, values, and habits (including buying habits). Teenagers are among the favorite demographic groups for advertisers. This is not because they like you! Instead, it is because they want to prey on the vulnerability of teenagers, many of whom are unsure about themselves. Advertisers also want to help teenagers establish life-long buying habits, because teenagers have many years of consumption ahead of them.

In this age of computers, companies go to a lot of trouble gathering demographic and psychographic information on consumers. For example, when one buys an MP3 player or a cell phone, it comes with a product registration card that asks questions about why one bought the product, when and how the buyer will use the product, what advertisements one may have seen about the product, what interests/hobbies the buyer has, even how much money the buyer makes. Many consumers ignore these cards, but others fill out all the information and mail them in.

Another technique used to gather information about consumers is the use of contests. Products aimed at teenagers often have contests that require people to reveal information similar to that asked for on the product registration card. Most people who enter the contest will not win, but the advertiser now has more information about people interested in its products. Sometimes, advertisers will run different types of advertisements at the same time to see which type of advertisement gets the most response. This is a question of **quantitative research,** because it examines the number (quantity) of people who respond to an advertisement. In a process referred to as **data mining,**

advertisers will examine the information they collect and see if different types of people respond to different types of advertisements. This is called **qualitative research,** because it examines types of people (their qualities) rather than simply the number of people who respond to an advertisement.

The activities in this section are designed to help you learn more about how advertisers design advertisements based on the needs and wants of different groups of consumers.

Tobacco Advertising and Teenagers - - - - - - - - - - - - - -

IN 1998, the largest U.S. tobacco companies settled a series of lawsuits with the governments of forty-six states and five U.S. territories. The tobacco companies agreed to pay approximately $206 billion over 25 years for tobacco prevention efforts. In an effort to reduce children's and teenagers' exposure to tobacco advertising, the settlement also required tobacco companies to take down all billboard advertising and advertising in sports arenas by 1999. By 2000, the tobacco companies promised to stop using cartoon characters to sell cigarettes and distributing "gear" such as shirts and hats with tobacco **logos.**

The settlement also saw tobacco companies agree to make many of their internal documents available to the public. One of these documents came from R.J. Reynolds, the maker of Camel, Kool, Pall Mall, and many other brands of cigarettes. (R.J. Reynolds makes about 30 percent of the cigarettes sold in the United States each year.) This document, written in 1973, was seen as one of the "smoking guns" by those who accused tobacco companies of intentionally directing advertising at teenagers, a claim that tobacco companies had repeatedly denied. In its discussion of "Psychological Effects," the R.J. Reynolds document says:

> The smoking-health controversy does not appear important to [teenagers] because, psychologically, at eighteen, one is immortal. Further, if the desire to be daring is part of the motivation to start smoking, the alleged risk of smoking may actually make smoking attractive.

> Finally, if the "older" establishment is preaching against smoking, the anti-establishment sentiment . . . would cause the young to want to be defiant and smoke. Thus a new brand aimed at the young group should not in any way be promoted as a "health" brand, and perhaps should carry some implied risk. In this sense, the warning label on the package may be a plus.

Suppose a tobacco company wanted to introduce a new cigarette brand called "The Dude's Deathsticks." The label of the package shows a skeleton with bloodshot eyes smoking a cigarette. In addition to the surgeon general's warning about the health risks of smoking (which are required by federal law), the package has a large warning that "These things will you kill you dead, my friend." Advertisements in magazines feature a picture of a grandmotherly-looking woman who looks upset, and who is quoted as saying "No kids of mine are going to smoke these things, and if they do, I'll give them a good whuppin'."

Consider the questions on the next page. Write your response in the space provided. Use another sheet of paper, if necessary.

1. Would you be interested in trying "The Dude's Deathsticks" cigarettes? Why or why not?

2. Do you think some of your friends would be interested in trying these cigarettes? Why or why not?

In 1971, cigarette advertisements on television were banned by federal law. Certainly, this policy has cost broadcasters many millions of dollars over the years, as cigarette companies spend a great deal of money on advertising.

3. If the federal government changed its mind and decided to allow cigarette advertisements on television, do you think some people who do not smoke might begin to? Explain.

4. Do you think that people who already smoke would smoke more if the federal government allowed cigarette advertisements on television? Explain.

Advertising at School- -

CONSIDER THE FOLLOWING questions. Write your response in the space provided. Use another sheet of paper, if necessary.

Look around your classroom. Count how many advertisements you can find. Examples include brand names on school supplies, computer and audio/visual equipment, and, of course, your clothing (and maybe the teacher's clothing).

1. How many advertisements did you find? List them.

2. How many advertisements did you find on clothing that are for the brand of that clothing?

3. How many advertisements did you find on clothing that are for things other than the brand of clothing? (This includes the names of colleges and sports teams.)

4. Why do people wear advertising?

5. Who is more likely to wear clothing with advertising—people your age, or people your parents' age? Why do you think this is the case? Explain.

Advertising and Problems:
"Let the Product Be the Hero" - - - - - - - - - - - - - - - - - -

ONE OF THE MOST common slogans among people in the advertising business is "let the product be the hero." One of the ways advertisers get us to buy things is to point out a problem consumers may have (whether real or imagined) and offer their product as a solution to that problem.

For example, an advertisement for a cleaning product may show pictures of a bathroom or kitchen before and after using the product. An advertisement for disposable diapers might emphasize that the product does not leak. Let's call these "physical" problems, because they are situations that involve some sort of physical change.

Other advertisements focus on personal or "social" problems. These include situations in which the advertised product is shown as helping the user avoid embarrassment, sadness, or loneliness. For example, the typical mouthwash advertisement talks about social problems associated with bad breath.

Consider the following questions. Write your response in the space provided. Use another sheet of paper, if necessary.

1. Find at least three advertisements that identify a problem, and examine how the advertised product is offered as a solution. Complete the chart.

Product	Problem	Solution

2. Think about each of the products and solutions in your chart. Is each situation realistic? Explain.

What Is the Advertisement Really Saying?--------

To HELP MAKE a product and its advertising memorable, many advertisements will rely on a slogan (also called a **tagline**). This is often presented at the end of a television or radio advertisement, or at the bottom of a newspaper or magazine advertisement. Examples include McDonald's "I'm Lovin' It" and Chevrolet's "An American Revolution."

Consider the following questions. Write your response in the space provided. Use another sheet of paper, if necessary.

1. Complete the chart. Name three advertising slogans and their product or company (other than McDonald's or Chevrolet). For each slogan, write what you think the slogan means (some will be easier to figure out than others).

Product	Slogan	Meaning

2. Look at your chart. Does the slogan make sense for each product? Explain why or why not.

Advertising and Age -

SENIOR CITIZENS ARE defined as people age 65 and older. Studies have shown that senior citizens watch more hours of television each week than the average teenager. However, very few advertisements on television are directed at senior citizens, while many advertisements are aimed at teenagers. Television shows and television networks that are aimed at teenagers are more attractive to advertisers than programs that are watched mostly by older adults. For example, even though *The Red Skelton Show* was the seventh most-watched show in the United States (and had been consistently in the top ten over the previous years), CBS cancelled it in 1970, because Skelton drew an older audience. In 1998, the highly popular program *Dr. Quinn, Medicine Woman* suffered the similar fate.

Consider the following questions. Write your response in the space provided. Use another sheet of paper, if necessary.

1. Why do you think advertisers are often less interested in older audiences?

2. Why do you think advertisers are more interested in teenagers?

3. Do you view advertisers' interest in you as a good thing or a bad thing? Explain.

Interview a senior citizen to learn what she or he thinks about advertising. Ask the following questions and record answers in the space below.

4. Why do you think advertisers are less interested in older audiences?

5. How do you feel about being less attractive to advertisers as you age?

Advertising and Ethnicity -

MOST PEOPLE WHO follow golf consider Tiger Woods to be the best golfer in the world today. Woods has broken racial and social barriers by succeeding in a sport that has historically been dominated by white men. Woods's mother is from Thailand and his late father was part African American. Woods has won golf tournaments at several country clubs where he cannot become a member because of his ethnicity.

Woods appeared in an advertisement for Buick cars several years ago. Buicks are luxury cars. Woods, who is in his early 30s, is less than half the age of the average Buick owner, who is older than 60. People who watch golf on television also tend to be older than the average television viewer. The average golf fan is also white, as is the average Buick owner.

Consider the following questions. Write your response in the space provided. Use another sheet of paper, if necessary.

1. Tiger Woods is partly black and in his 30s. The average Buick owner is white and older than 60. Why do you think Buick chose Woods to endorse its cars? Explain.

2. Do you think that ethnicity has a place in advertising? Why or why not? Explain.

3. Do you think that advertising can help break down social and racial stereotypes? Explain.

Celebrities and Advertising -

MANY PROFESSIONAL ATHLETES, who are paid millions of dollars to play football, tennis, and other sports, actually make much more money for appearing in advertisements for various products. These appearances in advertisements are referred to as endorsements. An endorsement means that the athlete is seen by consumers as saying the product is a good one. Sometimes the advertised product is related to the sport (for example, Serena Williams appearing in advertisements for tennis equipment, or LaDanian Tomlinson appearing in advertisements for athletic shoes). Sometimes, however, there is no relationship between sports and the product being advertised. (Tiger Woods appears in advertisements for Gillette razors, and Tomlinson appears in advertisements for AT&T.)

Obviously, the advertisers who pay athletes to endorse their products believe that these endorsements will sell more of their products.

Consider the following questions. Write your response in the space provided. Use another sheet of paper, if necessary.

1. Why do you think an advertisement featuring a professional athlete, for a product unrelated to sports, helps sell that product?

2. Besides athletes, what other types of celebrities appear in advertisements?

3. Consider some of your favorite athletes, musicians, and actors. Complete the chart below. Include at least two athletes, two musicians, and two actors. Next to each person, list a product that person endorses, if any.

Celebrity	Product

4. Does the fact that these people associate themselves with certain products make you more or less likely to buy the products? Explain.

5. Who ultimately ends up paying the money that athletes and other celebrities get for appearing in these advertisements? Explain.

Advertising and the Hierarchy of Needs - - - - - - - - - - -

ABRAHAM MASLOW was an American psychologist who studied people's needs. He identified certain categories of needs and ranked them. His rankings are referred to as **Maslow's Hierarchy of Needs.** (A **hierarchy** is a method of ranking things by degree of importance.)

Physiological needs come first. These are the most basic needs, such as food and water.

Safety comes next; this includes a sense of security. (This can include a feeling of financial security—the need to know that the bills are going to be paid.)

Social needs follow—these are needs that include love, acceptance by others, and the feeling of belonging.

Esteem is the next level. This means feeling respected by others and having self-respect.

At the top of Maslow's hierarchy is something he called **self-actualization.** This is the need to fulfill oneself, to become all that one is capable of being.

Maslow's Hierarchy of Needs is often shown as a pyramid, with the larger, lower levels representing the more basic needs, and the upper part representing the need for self-actualization.

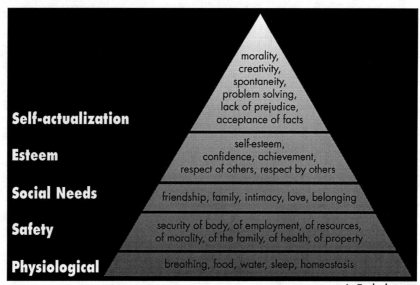

J. Finkelstein

Maslow said that if the needs that are lower in his hierarchy are not met, then it is very difficult or impossible to fulfill needs higher up in the rankings. (For example, if you were starving, would you have the time to worry about whether or not people thought you were cool?) It also becomes harder to meet the needs as one moves up the pyramid—food and water are easier to get than self-actualization.

Activity 8: Advertising and the Hierarchy of Needs *(continued)*

Using Maslow's Hierarchy of Needs, find five advertisements, each of which appeals to one of these needs in the consumer. If it is a magazine or newspaper advertisement, attach it to this page and label the need to which it appeals. If it is a television or radio advertisement, describe the advertisement.

1. Physiological needs—basic human needs such as food and water. Describe how the advertisement you have selected appeals to physiological needs.

2. Safety—the need to feel secure. Describe how the advertisement you have selected appeals to the need for safety.

3. Social needs—the need to feel loved and accepted. Describe how the advertisement you have selected appeals to social needs.

4. Esteem—the need to be respected by others and to have self-respect. Describe how the advertisement you have selected appeals to the need for esteem.

5. Self-actualization—the need to make the most of one's self in life. Describe how the advertisement you have selected appeals to the need for self-actualization.

Army Advertising -

THE FEDERAL GOVERNMENT is one of the largest advertisers in the United States. Most federal advertising is devoted to military recruiting, including recruiting for the U.S. Army. The last two Army advertising campaigns have focused on the taglines "Be All That You Can Be" (1981–2001) and "An Army of One" (2001–2006). In November 2006, the U.S. Army's advertising agency introduced the Army's new tagline, "Army Strong."

Although the previous two taglines focused on teenagers who were potential military recruits, the "Army Strong" campaign is directed more toward the parents of potential recruits. As the Army says, the current campaign "recognizes and respects the views of parents, family, friends, community members and employers and encourages the dialogue needed when making a life-changing decision."

Refer to the chart that discusses Maslow's Hierarchy of Needs in Activity 8. Use the chart to answer the following questions. Write your response in the space provided. Use another sheet of paper, if necessary.

1. Considering that the campaign was aimed at teenagers, to which of the needs on Maslow's chart do you think the "Be All That You Can Be" tagline was meant to appeal? Explain.

2. Do you think that this tagline is effective in appealing to that need? Explain.

3. Considering that the campaign was aimed at teenagers, to which of the needs on Maslow's chart do you think the "An Army of One" tagline was meant to appeal? Explain.

4. Do you think that this tagline is effective in appealing to that need? Explain.

5. Think of the "Army Strong" tagline, which appeals to parents. Which of the needs on Maslow's chart do you think parents have that this campaign addresses?

6. Why do you think that the Army switched its focus from potential recruits to the parents of those potential recruits? Explain.

7. Ask a parent what he or she thinks about the Army advertising aimed at parents. How does it make him or her feel? Explain.

8. How do you feel about the parent's response? Explain.

The objectives of this unit are to help students:

- understand how advertisers attempt to prey on consumers' self-esteem issues

- evaluate the pernicious effects of fashion advertising on a woman's body image

- recognize the pervasiveness of advertising in American culture

- assess the impact advertising has on women's health issues

- develop creative advertising approaches to social problems

In This Unit

What's the Message? requires students to scrutinize and deconstruct the language of advertising.

Consumption As Self-Expression? has students examine how advertisers appeal to teenagers' desire for autonomy.

Why Do Advertisers Want Us to Think That Thin Is In? allows students to evaluate the effect advertising has on a woman's body image.

So Many Shampoos! lets students assess firsthand the amount of advertising to which they have been exposed.

The Internet: The Next Frontier introduces students to the techniques by which Internet advertisers try to gather data about teenagers.

Cigarettes and Females has students examine the imagery of cigarette advertising and call on their own creativity to generate a response.

THE ROLE OF WOMEN in society has dramatically changed over the years. However, that is not always apparent in advertising. Much (but not all) of the advertising directed toward females presents women in stereotypical roles. Many advertisements show women who are worried about their looks and their weight, and who seem to obey males. Even though many females know that these messages are wrong, these messages are so frequent and widespread that it is almost impossible to ignore them.

Advertisers want people to buy things. If consumers are happy with life the way things are, then consumers are less likely to buy stuff. Advertisers know this, and so they subtly try to suggest that people are unhappy—unhappy with their appearance, relationships, homes, and with life in general—so that consumers will be more interested in buying advertised products that will "help." Advertisers offer their products as a solution to problems. If consumers do not know that they have a problem, then advertisers are more than happy to create one.

What's the Message? -

LOOK AT THREE advertisements for women's cosmetics or "beauty aids" in magazines such as *Seventeen*, *Glamour*, or *Cosmopolitan*.

Complete the following chart. Write your response in the space provided. Use another sheet of paper, if necessary.

What do these advertisements tell the audience is important in a female?

Product name	Message about females	Is this accurate? Explain.

Consumption As Self-Expression?----------------

ADVERTISEMENTS FOR TOMMY HILFIGER'S Tommy Girl perfume claim that the product is "a declaration of independence." Stetson's American Original perfume advertisements tell readers that "you have the right to be you," that you should "express your true self." The headline of an advertisement for Sanrio's Hello Kitty items says "Free to be me."

Consider the following questions. Write your response in the space provided. Use another sheet of paper, if necessary.

Look through women's fashion magazines. Find advertisements aimed at females your age that claim the advertised product helps or allows the consumer to be herself, to be one of a kind, to be special, or to express herself.

1. List three examples, listing the product and its advertising claim.

    a.

    b.

    c.

2. Why do you think this type of message is so common in advertising directed at teenagers? Explain.

3. Do you think this message is honest? Explain.

4. Do you think some people buy stuff because they think that stuff will tell other people something about them? Why or why not? Explain.

You or one of your friends has probably bought something, such as a type of clothing or a CD by a certain musician, because other friends had that item. This is an example of peer pressure.

Look through some magazines aimed at teenagers. Find three examples of advertisements that use peer pressure to try to sell a product. Note that sometimes the message is in the advertisement's words, and sometimes the message is in the picture(s). Try to find at least one example of each.

5. List the products, and describe next to each how the advertising uses peer pressure to sell that product.

a.

b.

c.

Why Do Advertisers Want Us to Think That Thin Is In? -

THE AVERAGE AMERICAN WOMAN is 5 feet 4 inches tall and weighs 142 pounds. The average fashion model is 5 feet 9 inches tall and weighs 110 pounds. More than 75 percent of American women say that they "feel fat."

Consider the following questions. Write your response in the space provided. Use another sheet of paper, if necessary.

1. How do you think magazine pictures of thin models make the average female reader feel about herself? Explain.

2. Explain how pictures of thin models, male or female, make you feel about yourself.

3. Why do you think advertisers usually choose thin models?

4. List three different types of advertisers who benefit from showing thin models. Explain the benefits for each advertiser.

Anorexia nervosa is a psychological illness that causes lack of appetite in people, primarily young women. Those who suffer from anorexia refuse to maintain body weight that is at or above the minimally normal weight for age and height. Bulimia nervosa is the practice of binge eating, often followed by forcing oneself to vomit.

5. Do you think that the constant use of abnormally thin fashion models by advertisers contributes to anorexia and bulimia? Explain.

So Many Shampoos!- -

CONSIDER THE FOLLOWING questions. Write your response in the space provided. Use another sheet of paper, if necessary.

1. Below, list all the brand names of hair shampoos that you can think of.

Take your list to a grocery store or drug store, and count how many brands of shampoo there are in the store.

2. How many brands did you find in the store? How many brands did you find that you named above? Underline them.

3. Why do you think there are so many different brands of shampoo?

4. Look on some of the back labels of different brands of shampoo—does a different company make every brand, or do some companies make many different brands?

Companies that make shampoo and other personal care products spend more than $5.7 billion on advertising each year, much of it aimed at teenagers.

5. What role do you think advertising plays in helping you to identify brands? Explain.

6. Why do you think most shampoo advertising is directed toward females? Explain.

The Internet: The Next Frontier — — — — — — — — — — — — — —

THERE ARE A VARIETY of Internet sites directed at female teenagers. These include gURL.com, ecrush.com, and vervegirl.com. Even though these sites are directed toward teenage females, each of these sites is actually put together by people who are 20- and 30-something years old. These sites rely on **cool hunting** to find out what teenage females are interested in, how they talk, and how advertisers can get their attention. Cool hunters interview teens online, at shopping malls, on the street, and near schools and social events. In short, they're hunting for what's "cool." They use the information they find to develop advertising campaigns aimed at teens.

Consider the following questions. Write your response in the space provided. Use another sheet of paper, if necessary.

1. Visit these Web sites, and describe three ways these Web sites try to be "cool."

    a.

    b.

    c.

Each of these is a commercial site that allows the visitor to become a member. When visitors join, the Web site's owner gathers information about those visitors.

2. How does offering the Web site as some sort of club make that Web site attractive to visitors? Explain.

Cigarettes and Females -

CIGARETTES HAVE LONG BEEN considered a no-calorie substitute for eating. The leading cigarette brand aimed at women, Virginia Slims, even highlights this in its name. One study at Harvard Medical School found that females who were unhappy about their appearance were twice as likely to think about using tobacco as females who were comfortable with their appearance.

The fact that cigarette advertisements frequently appear in fashion magazines that feature very thin fashion models certainly helps the cigarette industry.

Find three different advertisements in magazines that show cigarette smoking to be fashionable or even attractive. Remember, sometimes the message is in the words of the advertisement, and sometimes the message is in the pictures!

Consider the following questions. Write your response in the space provided. Use another sheet of paper, if necessary.

1. List the brand of cigarette in each advertisement. For each brand, describe how the advertisement makes smoking appear to be fashionable or attractive.

    a.

    b.

    c.

Cigarettes are a serious health hazard. Discussing health issues related to smoking may actually only encourage teenagers to smoke. Part of the problem may be, as with other examples we have seen, that people who are much older than teenagers are trying to learn how to be "cool" as they try to communicate with teenagers.

2. What do you think would be the best way to advertise to get teenagers to quit smoking? Where would you advertise? Explain.

3. Create an anti-smoking campaign.

    What would your advertisements show?

    What would be the words written, if any, in printed advertisements on television and in magazines, and the words said on television and radio advertisements?

    Use this space or another sheet of paper to plan your advertisement(s).

The objectives of this unit are to help students:

- understand how advertisers exploit ritualized traditional notions of manhood

- design and administer a survey, and tabulate the results

- examine how the literary device of personification is used in the advertising of products

- explore the concept of prestige pricing and the perceived need of many consumers to pay a premium for a product

- investigate the role of sports as a marketing device

- understand the practice of experimental marketing

In This Unit

Beer Drinking and Manhood lets students explore the use of masculine rituals as a theme of beer advertising.

Athletic Shoes Usually Aren't Cheap! introduces students to the concept of prestige pricing and helps students examine their own willingness to succumb to it.

Cigarettes, Brews, and Sports has students investigate the reasons cigarette and beer makers associate themselves with sports.

Are You Tough Enough to Drive a Truck? lets students evaluate the literary device of masculine personification in truck advertising.

Dealing with the Munchies is a suggested group project that allows students to create, administer, and tabulate a survey for a hypothetical new snack food.

Shaving and Experiential Marketing introduces students to the most recent trend in consumer product advertising.

Boys typically develop a definition of masculinity from older men who often serve as role models. Young males, like young females, are also influenced by society at large, including advertising. Children between the ages of 2 and 11 watch an average of 10 hours of television a week (and remember, most of them have to go to bed early). Television viewing varies from boy to boy, but the reality is that many American males learn what it means to be a man in part from advertising. As males get older, they begin reading magazines, often about sports, cars, and music, and other hobby-themed magazines. All of these magazines contain dozens of advertisements, usually aimed at men.

These advertisements are for such products as razors and shaving creams, alcohol, cars and trucks, and tobacco. Advertisements often offer the advertised product as a way to define oneself. If you look around, you will notice that many adults choose to buy cars or trucks that they believe reveal their personalities. For example, automakers found that many parents with children did not want to be seen as "old" and that they wanted to drive a vehicle that could hold the entire family but still look "cool." This is part of the reason that sport utility vehicles (SUVs) have become so popular. Notice that aftershave, a product often associated with men, rarely emphasizes how the product smells in advertisements; there is usually something else going on.

Beer Drinking and Manhood -------------------

BEER ADVERTISING is often associated with "guy" stuff—going to a football game, working at a construction site, shooting pool with friends, or even mowing the lawn. Beer advertisements often are set inside bars and clubs, with the implied message being that beer helps people have a good time. Beer-drinking men are often chatting with women in these ads. The message to men is: "Fun" is being accepted by the guys while also being attractive to the ladies.

Consider the following questions. Write your response in the space provided. Use another sheet of paper, if necessary.

Look for beer advertisements in magazines. Cut out an advertisement and attach it to this page.

1. How does the advertisement you selected try to appeal to a reader's sense of manhood?

2. Do you think beer companies believe that this is a good way to sell their product? Explain.

Find a print advertisement for a brand of beer, or watch some beer advertisements on television that use women to try to help sell that beer.

3. What connection is the intended audience supposed to make between the product and women?

4. Is that connection necessarily an intelligent one to make? Explain why or why not.

Athletic Shoes Usually Aren't Cheap! - - - - - - - - - - - -

CONSIDER THE FOLLOWING questions. Write your response in the space provided. Use another sheet of paper, if necessary.

1. Below, list all the brands of sneakers/athletic shoes that you can think of.

Take your list to a sporting goods store, and count how many brands of sneakers/athletic shoes there are in the store.

2. How many brands did you find in the store? How many brands did you find that you named above? Underline them.

3. Why do you think there are so many different brands of sneakers/athletic shoes?

4. What role do you think advertising played in helping you to identify brands? Explain.

5. Why do you think most sneaker/athletic shoe advertising is directed toward males? Explain.

Price is one of the main concerns of marketing. Prestige pricing means that the high price of an item brings a positive image not just to the product, but also to the person who buys the product. For example, some people drive a Lexus because they want people to know that they can afford to spend more than $50,000 on a car.

6. Prestige pricing is a major element of the marketing of many brands of athletic shoes. Explain why.

7. If you were going to buy a pair of shoes at a sporting goods store, would you try to find the least expensive pair? Explain.

8. Would you be willing to buy a no-name or unknown brand of athletic shoes if they were a few dollars less than the heavily advertised brands? Explain. What if they sold for about half the price of a popular brand? Explain.

9. If you pay more for a heavily advertised brand of shoe than an unadvertised brand, who is really paying for the cost of advertising that shoe? Explain your answer.

Cigarettes, Brews, and Sports - - - - - - - - - - - - - - - - - - -

EVEN THOUGH CIGARETTES AND BEER are not logically associated with sports, we have long seen those products advertised in sports settings. After the 1998 settlement between tobacco companies and forty-six states, cigarette advertising was removed from sports arenas and stadiums. Although cigarette advertising on television has been illegal for many years, anybody watching a televised athletic event probably saw numerous cigarette advertisements inside the arena or stadium, and most facilities today have advertisements for beer. For many years, Virginia Slims was the main sponsor of the professional Women's Tennis Association. For many years, R.J. Reynolds Tobacco Company sponsored the Winston Cup Series in NASCAR auto racing.

One NASCAR race is called the Budweiser Shootout. Kurt Busch drives a NASCAR racing car that advertises Miller Lite Beer. Major League Baseball's St. Louis Cardinals play at Busch Stadium, the Milwaukee Brewers play at Miller Field, and the Colorado Rockies play at Coors Field. Hockey's Montreal Canadiens once played in Le Centre Molson.

Many advertisements for beer often appear during telecasts of basketball games and other sporting events. In April 2008, a group of college presidents and athletic directors asked the National Collegiate Athletic Association (NCAA) to stop allowing beer advertisements to be shown during the NCAA's "March Madness" College Basketball Tournament. They said, "Alcohol ads demean the NCAA, student athletes, college [alcohol abuse] prevention efforts, and help put young people at risk."

1. Do you think that showing beer advertisements during college basketball games sends a bad message to young people? Explain.

2. Why do you think that some people are upset that beer, which contains alcohol, is associated with automobile racing, including NASCAR? Do you agree or disagree? Explain.

3. Why do you think that some people are upset that cigarettes are associated with some sports events? Do you agree or disagree? Explain.

4. Do you think that sponsorship of sporting events by beer and cigarette companies is a form of stealth marketing or not? Explain.

Are You Tough Enough to Drive a Truck?----------

Machismo is described as a strong, sometimes exaggerated masculinity. Machismo is displayed through physical strength, aggressiveness, and manliness. (*Macho* is a related word.)

Personification is the process in which one describes nonhuman objects in human terms. The United States flag is often referred to as "she." If a machine breaks down, people sometimes say, "He just doesn't want to run anymore," as if a machine can make choices. Both of these are examples of personification.

Advertising for most trucks is directed toward male consumers. Chevrolet trucks are "like a rock." Chevrolet tells consumers that its trucks are "hardworking" and "rugged." Ford trucks are "built Ford tough." Ford trucks are also "Dependable. Hardworking. Powerful. Capable." Ford's Web site tells consumers that knowledge about its trucks is a sign of the consumer's machismo. Dodge trucks are "tough" and "powerful." Dodge tells consumers that its Ram is "one of the biggest, strongest and hardest-working trucks anywhere." Toyota asks consumers if they consider themselves "tough enough for Tacoma?" Nissan describes its trucks as "tough" and their styling "aggressive."

Consider the following questions. Write your response in the space provided. Use another sheet of paper, if necessary.

1. Explain why you think truck advertising uses personification.

2. Explain why you think truck advertising emphasizes macho-type qualities.

Activity 4: Are You Tough Enough to Drive a Truck? *(continued)*

Over the last few years, car companies have been selling more and more trucks to women. Some companies, such as Ford, have asked women to tell them what features they want in trucks.

Imagine that Ford wanted to sell trucks to both men and women, without offending either gender.

3. Would you change the way Ford advertises its trucks, or leave its advertising the way it is? Explain.

Dealing with the Munchies -

MARKETING RESEARCH HAS SHOWN that teenage males spend the biggest percentage of their money on food and entertainment, while teenage girls spend the biggest percentage of their money on cosmetics and clothing.

Consider the following questions. Write your response in the space provided. Use another sheet of paper, if necessary.

1. Find three advertisements for food products that you believe are aimed at teenage males. List the products, and next to each, explain why you think the advertisement is aimed specifically at teenage males.

Product name	Why teenage males? Explain.

Frito-Lay, the maker of Fritos, Doritos, Ruffles, and other brands of chips, is owned by the same company that makes Pepsi. This makes sense when you think about the fact that most people want something cold to drink when eating chips.

Frito-Lay's Doritos are primarily directed at teenagers. Although more male teenagers buy chips than female teenagers, females are still considered an important part of the market. Doritos advertisements had appeared for years during the Super Bowl, but in 2002, Frito-Lay discontinued the advertisements. The company's research showed that many teenagers now view the Internet as more important to them than television, so Frito-Lay has tripled the amount of money it spends advertising on the Internet and continues to do so.

2. Do you think it was a good idea for Frito-Lay to discontinue its Doritos advertisements during the Super Bowl and shift the money to Internet advertising? Why or why not? Explain.

Go to frito-lay.com and read about the many different flavors and brands of chips the company makes. In order for Frito-Lay to continue to grow as a company, it is constantly looking for new chip products to introduce. Before introducing a new type of chip, Frito-Lay does lots of test marketing to see what flavor and style of chip gets the best results.

3. Imagine that Frito-Lay is going to introduce a new type of chip. Since teenagers are the company's target **demographic,** it asks you to survey students in your school and find out what the new flavor or style of chip should be.

It will probably be easier to do this as a group project.

Before you begin, consider the questions on the next page.

What type of questions are you going to ask?

Consider which of these options is best for your survey (you may stick to one type of question or a combination):

- **Open-ended questions** allow the students who respond to the survey to express their own feelings and opinions about a new chip. However, open-ended questions presume that people actually have feelings and opinions on the subject, and that they can express them in words—this is not always the case. After asking all your respondents an open-ended question, you need to sit down and see what the most common responses are. In other words, if you asked 100 people what new kind of chip they wanted, and 3 said an extra salty chip, and 45 said they would like a sweet chip with cinnamon on it, which type of chip would you recommend?

- **Close-ended questions** can be answered with "yes" or "no." There can be more than two choices, but the choices are always provided by the person asking the questions. The respondent then chooses his or her answer from those choices. The problem here is that you may not be giving the respondent a chance to tell what he or she really wants or does not want, since you are creating the answers for him or her. To tabulate answers to close-ended questions, you simply count the number of people who responded to each given choice of answers.

- **Likert scale questions** use a numbered scale, such as from 1 to 5, or 1 to 10. For example, a question that asked about how spicy somebody wanted a new chip to be could use 1 for "not spicy at all" to 10 for "so spicy it's scary." The advantage of a Likert scale is that it allows you to arrive at a numerical average. ("Of 100 people surveyed, they said they liked a spiciness level that averaged 6.3 on a 10-point scale.") The problem with this type of question is the same as with other close-ended questions—you are limiting the types of responses a person can give you.

How many questions are you going to ask? Too many will bore your respondents after a while. Too few might mean you do not ask all the questions you should.

How many people are you going to ask? Since this is not a professional survey, you will not have the opportunity to ask nearly as many people as Frito-Lay would in a real survey, which might include hundreds of people in different parts of the country.

Finally, what are the questions you are going to ask? List them on a separate sheet, making certain that you explain what type of question each question is—open-ended, close-ended, or Likert scale.

Administer your survey at your school. Tabulate your results and report your findings. Discuss with your class.

Shaving and Experiential Marketing - - - - - - - - - - - - - - -

MARKETING RESEARCH HAS SHOWN that most American females view shaving their legs and underarms as a necessary but unpleasant routine. This is partly due to females' perception that having hair on their legs and underarms is not feminine. Men, however, have been found to actually enjoy shaving, in part because having facial hair is a sign of masculinity. For men, shaving seems to be a ritual of manhood rather than a chore. In this view, shaving proves that a man is indeed a man, and good grooming proves that he is a respectable man.

As a result of these findings, manufacturers of shaving products offer their products to men as much more than a blade and some soap. Instead, advertisements for men's shaving products emphasize that those products allow men to enjoy the experience of being a man. This is called **experiential marketing.** In this kind of marketing, the advertiser emphasizes the experience a consumer will have rather than the product itself.

Consider the following questions. Write your response in the space provided. Use another sheet of paper, if necessary.

1. Find three advertisements directed toward males, either in print or on television, that emphasize their product as part of a celebrated male ritual. List three products in the chart. List the words or images used in the advertisements, and describe how those words or images portray a celebration of manliness.

Product name	Key words/images	How manly?

Many other products rely on experiential marketing. Pepsi created an advertisement in which Faith Hill sang a song about the "Joy of Cola." Nothing was said about the product itself. The message of the advertisement was that the consumer's act of drinking Pepsi is a fun experience.

2. Find three advertisements for products that rely on experiential marketing that are directed at both men and women. List the three products. Next to each, list the words or images used in the advertisements, and describe how those words or images emphasize the user's experience with the product rather than something about the product itself.

Product name	Key words/images	Experience emphasized?

The objectives of this unit are to help students:

- understand how visual and auditory imagery is constructed and manipulated in order to engage consumers

- develop awareness of the use of a boycott as a social and economic strategy

- use the Internet to research business transactions

- understand how advertisers use marketing research to refine their messages

MANY OF THOSE WHO TEACH today comment on what is seen as the increasing diminution of students' attention spans, and the perception that students are becoming increasingly visual learners. It can be argued that today these characteristics describe the American public in general. This unit discusses how television and radio advertising have contributed to these phenomena; ironically, television and radio advertisers actively search for ways to battle these phenomena in their efforts to attract the American public's attention.

In This Unit

The Hard Cut allows students to investigate the ways in which television advertisers attract and maintain consumers' attention through editing techniques and construction of visual imagery.

Lights! Cameras! Tunes! has students investigate the role of music in television and radio advertising.

Television Commercials and Setting provides students with a method of analyzing how the setting of commercials can evoke certain attitudes among consumers.

MTV and You re-introduces students to the practice of "cool hunting." Students will discover how a television network completely focused on teenaged viewers develops its programming, and the role marketing plays in MTV programming.

The Boycott has students evaluate the effectiveness and the ethical aspects of boycotts by advocacy groups against television advertisers.

Product Placement and Positive Attitudes introduces students to the subtle and effective use of product placement within television programs.

Your Name Here requires students to do some basic Internet research, as they search for information about the money advertisers pay for naming rights on stadiums and arenas. Students also evaluate the effectiveness of the millions of dollars spent on these naming rights.

What's the Best Advertisement on Television? asks students to identify a particularly effective advertisement and explain its effectiveness.

Radio and Demographics has students distinguish the musical tastes of different age groups and different genders, and requires them to estimate what types of products will be directed to these different groups. Students check their estimates empirically.

COMMERCIAL RADIO STATIONS began broadcasting in the United States in the 1920s. Commercial television stations began broadcasting in the 1940s. By "commercial" we mean radio and television stations that rely on advertisers to make a profit. These stations must pay their employees, pay for their electronic equipment, pay for their buildings, and pay for the programming they broadcast, while not charging listeners for the entertainment provided.

Radio and television broadcasters attempt to appeal to certain **demographic** audiences. Once an audience has been gathered, salespeople for the broadcaster seek advertisers who are interested in advertising to that station's audience. Modern television advertising shows a trend toward shorter advertisements, with lots of **hard cuts** (rapid shifting from one image to another) and the use of music. In general, the pacing of television advertising has continually sped up over the past 40 years. Old television and radio advertisements would sometimes last a minute or more; now, there are many advertisements that last only 10 seconds.

Radio advertising is usually done by local businesses, such as stores, restaurants, and clubs, although some national advertisers also run advertisements on radio. Radio advertising is very inexpensive, compared with other media such as television. This is because the cost to make a radio advertisement is low. All a radio advertisement needs is one or two voices, maybe with some sound effects or music. The price charged by radio stations to run an advertisement is also relatively cheap. Because the advertisements are inexpensive,

those who advertise on radio can afford to emphasize **frequency**—one may hear many advertisements for the same advertiser, or may hear the same advertisement repeatedly. This emphasis on frequency can also be explained by the fact that many of us pay very little attention to what is being said on the radio.

Advertisers know this, so they often rely on repetition. Although one or two advertisements for a particular product may not get our attention, hearing advertisements for the same product dozens of times over the course of a week helps get the advertiser's message across.

Many people listen to the radio in their cars, on the way to and from work or school. The highest radio listenership occurs during so-called "drive time"—during the morning and evening rush hours (7 to 9 A.M., 4 to 6 P.M.). Many advertisements try to appeal to people who might make impulsive decisions on the road—for example, for a fast-food restaurant, a coffee place, a convenience store, and so on.

During the early years of radio, each radio station tried to aim itself at all listeners. With the introduction of television in the late 1940s, radio stations changed their approach. Today, different radio stations appeal to different demographic groups, in order to deliver particular audiences to advertisers. As a result, we have radio stations with music formats such as "smooth jazz," "album-oriented rock," "soft adult contemporary," "adult contemporary," "alternative rock," "rhythmic pop," and "classic rock."

Ad Buzz *(continued)*

There are more than 4,700 commercial radio stations on the AM band and more than 6,000 stations on the FM band in the United States. The great majority of these radio stations rely on advertising for their income. In 2006, American radio station owners received more than $10 billion from advertisers.

There are more than 1,300 commercial broadcast television stations in the United States, in addition to numerous cable channels. Just as most radio stations do, most television stations (with the exception of premium channels, such as HBO and pay-per-view) rely on advertising to make a profit. Television rates vary greatly, depending on the size of the audience watching a particular program at a particular time. For example, a 30-second advertisement on a local television station in a small town might cost the advertiser only a few hundred dollars. But consider that a 30-second advertisement on *American Idol* costs $780,000. CBS charged $2.6 million for 30-second advertisements during the 2008 Super Bowl. Altogether, advertisers spent $65 billion on television advertising in 2008.

The Hard Cut- -

IN ADDITION TO THE MONEY spent to obtain commercial time on television stations, advertisers spend many millions of dollars producing the commercials that they will broadcast. Many advertisements today contain attention-getting special effects. These include computer-generated imagery and animation, unusual camera angles, and lots of hard cuts. A hard cut occurs when the televised image or scene on the screen abruptly changes to another, possibly very different, image.

To enhance the effect of hard cuts, there are also more images or scenes being shown in the typical television advertisement than was the case in the past. A 30-second television advertisement 20 years ago may have had only one or two cuts. Today, a 30-second advertisement may have dozens of hard cuts.

For example, imagine a 30-second television advertisement for a vacation resort in Mexico or the Caribbean. The first scene may be of a couple talking about their vacation while inside their living room at home. The scene may move back and forth between the living room and multiple shots of the couple doing different things at the advertised resort: water-skiing, playing golf, sitting on the beach, dancing in a club, eating at a fancy restaurant.

Watch five 30-second television advertisements for different types of products. Write down how many different "cuts" there are in each advertisement. (You may find this easier to do with the sound turned down.)

Record your answers below. Use another sheet of paper, if necessary.

1. Write down the number of cuts you counted for each advertisement.

Product name	Number of cuts

2. Now calculate the average number of cuts for the five advertisements you watched.

3. Why do you think television advertisements have so many hard cuts?

4. Ask an older adult how she or he feels about these types of advertisements. Does the adult find these types of advertisements exciting or confusing? Explain.

5. Ask that older adult why she or he feels this way.

Lights! Cameras! Tunes! -

IN THE 1950s AND 1960s, radio and television advertisements often relied on jingles. **Jingles** are short little songs especially written for an advertisement, which usually name the product in the song and contain lyrics about the value of that product. Jingles are relatively inexpensive and are still used in many advertisements today, but advertisers have begun to rely more heavily on popular songs that have previously been performed by well-known artists. For example, Microsoft paid the Rolling Stones $12 million to use their song "Start Me Up" when the company introduced Windows 95. The legal rights to many old Beatles songs were actually owned for several years by Michael Jackson. Jackson angered some of the former Beatles by selling the rights to some of those songs to several advertisers for use in television advertisements, including the use of the song "Revolution" in advertisements for Nike shoes.

Many current musicians, such as Shakira, John Legend, Badly Drawn Boy, Justin Timberlake, and Jay-Z, have sold the right to use their music in advertisements.

Consider the following questions. Write your response in the space provided. Use another sheet of paper, if necessary.

1. Complete the chart. List three advertisers that use jingles in television or radio advertisements. Next to each advertiser you listed, write whether you think the jingle helps sell the product or not. Explain your thinking.

Product	Is the jingle effective?	Explain

2. Complete the chart. List three advertisers that use popular songs in television or radio advertisements. Next to each advertiser you listed, write the name of the song used in the advertising. Do you think the song was effective? Explain.

Product	Song	Is the song effective?	Explain

3. Why do you think that advertisers are willing to pay much more money to use popular songs in their advertisements, instead of paying much less money for jingles?

4. Is this a good or a bad idea on the part of advertisers? Explain.

Television Commercials and Setting- - - - - - - - - - - - -

THE LOCATION OF WHERE the activity occurs in a television commercial is called the setting. For example, the setting for a food product may be the kitchen where it is prepared, the dining room where it is eaten, the store where it is purchased, or maybe the farm where it is grown. The people who produce television advertisements pay a great deal of attention to setting. This is because television commercials rely heavily on visual images to sell the product. Sometimes the settings are typical—they look like the sort of place where one would expect the product to be used. Sometimes the settings are atypical—the people who make the commercial choose unusual settings to get our attention, or to create a "mood" about the product.

Consider the following questions. Write your response in the chart on the page provided. Use another sheet of paper, if necessary.

Watch three television advertisements for cars and other vehicles. Make sure that at least one of the advertisements is for a sport utility vehicle (SUV) or a truck.

1. List the brand of each advertised vehicle.

2. Describe the setting of each advertisement—in the city, the suburbs, or the countryside.

3. Explain why you think the setting for each was chosen.

4. Were the vehicles portrayed as going fast or slow?

5. What types of audio were used? Did the ads use the noise the car makes, music, or a voice-over?

6. Describe the audio for each ad. If the ad used music, did the music relate to the speed? If so, describe how. If the ad had a voice-over, summarize what was said.

Vehicle name	Setting description	Explain the setting choice	Fast or slow?	Type of audio	Describe the audio

Many advertisers today emphasize **experiential marketing.** This means that they don't focus on the product being sold, but how the product can make the consumer feel.

Now think about the ads you watched.

7. Is the information given about each vehicle mostly facts about the car—price, engine size, number of passengers—or about "attitude"? Explain.

8. Do you think that information given about each vehicle is important to the type of person who would buy that vehicle? Explain.

Take another look at the use of mood in advertisements. Watch three television advertisements for long-distance telephone service or for cell-phone service. Try watching with the sound turned down.

9. Describe the faces of the people shown in the advertisement.

10. Do people always feel this way when using long-distance service or a cell phone? Why are people shown this way? Explain.

Most soft drink advertisements do not talk about how the product tastes. Many people say that these advertisements are really trying to sell a positive attitude about the product—that thinking it is "cool" to drink a certain brand of soda is more important than how the product tastes.

11. Do you agree or disagree with this statement? Why?

MTV and You -

YOU ARE A MEMBER of the key demographic group that MTV works hard to appeal to. MTV uses some of its employees to do **cool hunting.** Cool hunters go out into different communities to talk to teenagers about what trends are popular at the moment and what's not. Using this research, MTV tries to create programs that viewers will think are cool, so that more viewers will watch them. MTV shares some of the information it finds with the companies that advertise on MTV so that advertisers can make commercials that are also considered cool.

Get a stopwatch, such as the stopwatch feature on many cell phones. A digital kitchen timer will work, too. Watch MTV for an hour. Consider the following questions. Write your response in the space provided. Use another sheet of paper, if necessary.

1. Count how many advertisements you see during that hour (count music videos, if any, as advertisements for record companies). Record your answer:

2. Count how many products, if any, are identified by name during the programs, as opposed to during advertisements (this includes the name of a new CD, a new video, or a new movie). Record your answer:

3. How many minutes of the hour were devoted to various forms of advertising activity, including commercials and the naming of products during the programs? Record your answer:

4. Do the math—what percentage of the hour was devoted to various forms of advertising activity? Record your answer:

5. Can commercials be "cool"? Explain.

6. Are there some ads that you actually enjoy watching? Which ones? Explain what you like about them.

The Boycott------------------------------------

A BOYCOTT IS THE ACT OF refusing to do business with an organization because people believe it has done something wrong, or is currently doing something wrong. The goal of a boycott is either to punish a business for what it has done wrong, or to put pressure on that business to change its practices.

Sometimes different groups of people take up a boycott, or at least threaten one, that is directed toward television advertisers. These groups may be mad at the advertiser itself, perhaps for showing an advertisement that is considered insulting or shocking to some people. Sometimes these groups are mad at the television shows during which an advertiser runs its commercials. The strategy is, if advertisers know that some people will not buy products advertised during certain television shows, then the advertisers will either put pressure on the television network to change the show or the network will lose the advertisers' business.

In 2008, some Americans, upset over human rights violations they believed were caused by, or allowed by, the Chinese government in Tibet and Darfur, asked advertisers not to place advertisements on NBC's broadcasts of the Summer Olympics in Beijing. However, there seemed to be little response to the boycott request from advertisers, who went ahead with plans to advertise during the Olympics.

Years before, the American Family Association (AFA) pressured advertisers to stop running commercials during *Saturday Night Live.* The AFA argued that the show had too much sexual content and made fun of Christian beliefs. Some boycotts are directed toward advertisers rather than television shows. The AFA later urged shoppers to boycott Target stores for referring to "the holidays" rather than "Christmas" in its November and December television advertising.

Not all television advertiser boycotts deal with sexual or religious issues. For example, the National Association for the Advancement of Colored People, the Media Action Network for Asian-Americans, the National Hispanic Foundation for the Arts, and other groups were angered when the 1999 television season introduced twenty-six new shows, none of which had a person of color in a leading role. After the groups threatened a boycott of network television, ABC, CBS, NBC, and Fox all agreed to create more ethnic diversity on their programs. Some Italian-American groups have objected to the frequent representation of Italian-Americans as members of organized crime. Other boycotts have been directed at advertisers for airing advertisements that were seen as racially insensitive.

Some people argue that most advertising is a "one-way street" because advertisers tell us whatever they want, but consumers usually do not have the chance to talk back. These people say that regardless of the message (in this case, the reason for the boycott), it is important that people are allowed to organize a boycott, even if you personally disagree with a particular message.

Consider the following questions. Write your response in the space provided. Use another sheet of paper, if necessary.

1. Do you believe a boycott of advertisers is a good way to make television companies more respectful of a certain group of people? Explain.

Sometimes, the advertiser itself is the target of a boycott. For example, an advertisement for the Toyota RAV4 portrayed an African-American man in a manner that some African-American groups found insulting. The threatened boycott caused Toyota to discontinue the advertisement and publicly apologize.

2. Do you believe a boycott of an advertiser is a good way to make that advertiser more respectful of a certain group of people? Explain.

3. Some people argue that a boycott of television programs or advertisers is a form of censorship. Do you agree? Explain.

Product Placement and Positive Attitudes --------

ADVERTISERS ARE CONCERNED about the fact that many of us watch television with a remote control in our hand. They worry that when advertisements come on we switch channels. As a result, advertisers are putting more attention today into the practice of product placement. This means that advertisers will pay the producers of television programs to show the characters on those programs using the advertisers' products. The character who uses the product, of course, is one that viewers are supposed to like. In most cases, you will not see a bad guy use the "placed" product! Some of the products that have been placed in programs include Diet Coke and Heinz ketchup.

Consider the following questions. Write your response in the space provided. Use another sheet of paper, if necessary.

1. If you were an advertiser, would you think that product placement is a good idea or a bad idea? Explain.

2. Complete the chart. Name three television programs you watch. For each show, name a product (by brand, such as *Coke,* or by product type, such as *soft drink*) that would be a good item to place on the program. Explain why you think that program would be a good fit for placing that product.

Program title	Product	Explain placement

3. As a consumer, do you think product placement is a good idea or a bad idea? Explain.

The federal government is also involved in product placement—sort of. A few years ago, Congress decided to spend federal money to insert anti-drug-abuse messages in programs popular with teenagers. Congress agreed to spend $1 billion over five years, on the condition that the networks give the government a significant discount on advertising prices.

4. Do you think using taxpayers' money to have fictional television characters talk against drug abuse is a good idea or a bad idea? Explain.

5. In the case of most product placement, advertisers are trying to sell a product, such as a food product or a brand of clothing. In the case of the government's anti-drug-abuse campaign, the government is trying to sell an idea or an attitude—"drug abuse is bad." What do you think is harder to sell, a product or an attitude? Explain.

Your Name Here -

MANY OF THE SPORTING EVENTS on television have a corporate sponsor. For example, professional golf tournaments include the Sony Open and the Kraft Nabisco Championship. College bowl games in December and January are frequently named after companies, such as the Allstate Sugar Bowl. The arenas and stadiums in which televised games are played usually have dozens of advertisements located throughout the building. In fact, although cigarette companies are not allowed to advertise on television, until recently one could still see advertisements for cigarettes that were inside sports arenas and stadiums when watching televised games.

Many stadiums and arenas in which professional sports teams play also have companies' names in their titles. This is not because those companies own those stadiums and arenas. Instead, the owners sell the "naming rights" to those buildings. Naming rights are considered a part of a company's advertising, and many companies are willing and eager to spend many millions of dollars for that right.

Consider the following questions. Write your response in the space provided. Use another sheet of paper, if necessary.

1. List and describe three benefits that a company receives by paying for the naming rights to a stadium or an arena.

2. Do you believe that these reasons are good enough to justify spending millions of dollars? Explain.

Sometimes, the arena or stadium that has its naming rights sold to a private company is actually owned by the public. In other words, the community's taxpayers paid to build the building, but a private company paid to have its name put on that building.

3. Do you think this is a good idea or a bad idea? Why? Explain.

Sometimes the money that is paid to name a public stadium goes to the people who own the team instead of the community that owns the stadium. This practice is defended by some people, who say that the owner of the team can use the money to get better players.

4. Do you think this is a good idea or a bad idea? Why? Explain.

In 1999, the energy company Enron agreed to pay $100 million over 30 years for the naming rights for the Houston Astros' new baseball stadium. Two years later, Enron became widely known for a huge financial scandal. The company went bankrupt, thousands of people lost their jobs, and government authorities began investigating possible criminal activity.

5. If you were the owner of the Houston Astros, what would you do in this situation? Explain.

The rest of this activity requires some Internet research.

6. Find out on the Internet what the owner of the Astros did. Summarize your findings.

7. Do you think he made the right decision? Why or why not? Explain.

Research the names of the three stadiums or arenas nearest you where professional sports teams play.

8. Write down the names of those three stadiums or arenas.

9. For each stadium named after a company, find out how much the company paid for the naming rights and how long the contract is for. Record your findings here.

What's the Best Advertisement on Television? - - - -

SOME PEOPLE HAVE SAID that advertisements are often the best entertainment on television. Television advertising certainly is the result of a lot of hard work by some very talented people. These advertisements usually have what advertisers refer to as a "call to action." Advertisers try to get television viewers' attention and try to get viewers to want a product or service, or at least want to learn more about a product. They have to do this within a fraction of a minute; some advertisements are only 10 seconds long. Television advertisements may include famous celebrities, interesting special effects, or humor, all designed to grab our attention.

Consider the following questions. Write your response in the space provided. Use another sheet of paper, if necessary.

1. What do you think is the best advertisement on television now? Explain. Name the product and describe the ad.

2. What is this advertisement's call to action—what does the advertisement want you to do after you see the advertisement? Explain.

3. Is the advertisement effective as a call to action—does it make you want to do something? Explain.

4. Can an advertisement be entertaining but not be effective? Explain.

Radio and Demographics -

TELEVISION BROADCASTERS and radio broadcasters both try to develop an audience for their stations through programming. Television broadcasters choose programs that will attract a certain type of audience. For example, football games will attract a mostly male audience. Soap operas will attract mostly female viewers. Cartoons are aimed at young children. Radio broadcasters develop their audiences through the type of music they play. Oldies stations are aimed at older adults, stations that play lots of rap and hip-hop are aimed at teenagers, more males listen to heavy metal than females, and so on.

This exercise is exactly what radio stations try to do—identify a "sound" that attracts a particular type of listener and find advertisers who want to appeal to that type of listener. Consider the following questions. Write your response in the chart on the next page. Use another sheet of paper, if necessary.

1. List five local radio stations. Make sure to include your favorite and that of an adult in your household.

2. Listen to each station for about 5 minutes. Indicate the age group the station tries to reach. Use the following categories to complete the chart: 12–18, 18–24, 24–34, 34–45, 45 and older.

3. Many, but not all, stations direct themselves at primarily one gender. Which gender do you think that station is primarily aimed at—men or women, or both?

4. What types of advertisers would want to appeal to those groups? Write your ideas in the chart.

5. Now listen again to each of the five stations for about 15 minutes or until you've heard several advertisements on each station. List these advertisers in the chart. Were you right or wrong about the types of advertisers that you thought would advertise on that station?

Activity 9: Radio and Demographics (continued)

Radio station	Target ages	Target gender	Who I think would advertise	Who does advertise

Media Literacy: Advertising

The objectives of this unit are to help students:

- identify the persuasive and attention-getting techniques employed in print advertising

- understand demographic and psychographic differences in American society

- evaluate the arguments of those who want to regulate certain forms of advertising and those who do not

- develop a process for decision making that requires evaluating information and identifying what additional information is needed before making an informed decision

PRINT ADVERTISING IS PROBABLY the easiest form of advertising to study in a classroom setting. It is recommended that students bring in some of their own favorite magazines, as well as local newspapers. One can also easily obtain magazines that pertain to very specific interests and activities, such as weddings, various hobbies and occupations, and so on.

Depending on where your school is located, your students may or may not have been exposed to a significant number of billboards and transit advertising on taxis and buses. The activities that discuss outdoor advertising do not require that the student have significant exposure to outdoor advertising.

In This Unit

What Catches Your Eye? requires students to select the three most attention-getting advertisements in a magazine and analyze the visual and thematic aspects of each advertisement.

Different Magazines, Different Advertisements helps students to distinguish between advertisements for low-involvement items (items that usually require little thought before buying) and advertisements for high-involvement items that require more thought.

Something for Everybody has students assess demographic and psychographic differences among different magazines.

Bad Billboards—A Bad Influence? asks students to evaluate the impact of tobacco and alcohol advertising in disadvantaged neighborhoods. This exercise also lets students evaluate the role of government in regulating advertising.

Bad Billboards Everywhere? introduces students to the arguments made by groups that oppose billboards along roadways and groups that support billboards. Students must then identify and summarize the key points of each argument and explain which side they find most persuasive.

Teacher Buzz *(continued)*

Newspapers versus Magazines: You Decide has students simulate one of the frequent decisions made by advertising agencies—which medium to purchase advertising in, and why. Students are asked to compare the relative advantages and disadvantages of two competing media, and are then asked to identify what additional information they would need to know before making an informed decision.

PRINT ADVERTISING CAN (but does not always) provide more information than most other advertising formats. Print advertising is static. It does not move. People (and other animals) are attracted to movement, so print advertising uses various techniques to get our attention. For example, an ad on the right-hand page of a newspaper or magazine (called the **recto** side in the advertising business) usually costs more than the same size ad on the left-hand (**verso**) side. This is because readers of English use the Roman alphabet (as compared with the Arabic or Japanese alphabets, for example). Since written words in English move from left to right, a reader of English naturally moves his or her eyes toward the right when going through the simple motion of turning through a newspaper or a magazine. Similarly, it is natural for the eye to take a reader from the top left side of the page and move down to the bottom right-hand side of the page. As a result, most newspaper and magazine advertisements are loosely arranged in the form of the letter *Z*, taking a reader's eyes across the information the advertiser wants to show.

Beauty for the Eye of the Beholder

Advertisements in magazines rely very heavily on color photography to get consumers' attention. The objects in the photographs are carefully arranged to be as eye-catching as possible. Photographs of fashion models in advertisements for personal care products such as cosmetics and shampoo are almost always airbrushed to remove any blemishes on the model. Today, more and more photographs are digitally altered. This allows the photographer to put in or take out anything he or she decides to. As a result, blemishes can be removed, hair and eye color can be changed, and lips can be made fuller.

About 60 percent of a typical newspaper is devoted to advertising. Newspapers usually contain more localized advertisements for local stores, services, and so forth. Some of this advertising is actually designed by the advertiser itself, as opposed to an advertising agency. As a result, some of the advertising may appear to be less sophisticated than ads created by professionals at advertising agencies.

Who's Advertising? Who's Looking?

Different readers favor different sections of the newspaper. Advertisements aimed primarily at men often appear in the sports section. Advertisements aimed primarily at women often appear in the living, life, lifestyle, or home section (the title depends on the newspaper).

In some ways, billboards require advertisers to use the opposite approach of what is used in much print advertising. Magazine and newspaper advertisements can provide a lot of information. Billboards have to get their message across quickly. Billboards are typically along major roadways, designed to get the attention of motorists and their passengers as they drive by. The billboard industry says that a billboard advertisement, to be effective, must communicate its information within 6 to 10 seconds. Thus, billboard advertisers pay careful attention to how few words can be used to communicate a message, what colors are most attractive and most easily read, what kinds of lettering are easiest to read, and what sort of photographs or drawings can be included to help get the message across quickly to the consumer.

What Catches Your Eye? -

LOOK AT ALL THE ADVERTISEMENTS in one magazine. Find the three advertisements that get your attention the most, cut them out, and attach them to this page.

Consider the following questions. Write your response in the space provided. Use another sheet of paper, if necessary.

1. For each advertisement, explain why it caught your attention.

   Ad 1:

   Ad 2:

   Ad 3:

2. For each advertisement, describe the visual composition of the advertisement. Consider any attention-getting elements such as color or image. Explain.

   Ad 1:

   Ad 2:

   Ad 3:

Activity 1: What Catches Your Eye? *(continued)*

3. Is the type of lettering attention-getting? Explain.

Ad 1:

Ad 2:

Ad 3:

4. Is the way the pictures, drawings, and words are arranged on the page attention-getting? Explain.

Ad 1:

Ad 2:

Ad 3:

5. For each advertisement, describe the theme or subject of the advertisement. Is the theme unusual for the type of product being advertised? (For example, using a photograph of a kid on a skateboard to sell a computer—most people would not automatically connect the two.) Explain.

   Ad 1:

   Ad 2:

   Ad 3:

6. Is the language used in the wording attention-getting? Explain.

   Ad 1:

   Ad 2:

   Ad 3:

7. Does the advertisement suggest a certain attitude that the advertiser has, or that the consumer has? Explain.

   Ad 1:

   Ad 2:

   Ad 3:

Different Magazines, Different Advertisements - - -

SOME ADVERTISED PRODUCTS ARE low-involvement items that one may frequently use without putting much thought into. For example, when was the last time you stopped and thought about a soft drink? High-involvement items are often more expensive items, or items that require significant emotional investment. For example, if you were shopping for a car, would you be likely to buy the first one you see?

Look at advertisements in a business magazine such as *Fortune, Forbes, Business Week,* and *The Economist.* Now look at advertisements in fashion magazines such as *Glamour* or *GQ,* and advertisements in sports and entertainment magazines such as *Sports Illustrated* and *Spin.*

Consider the following questions. Write your response in the space provided. Use another sheet of paper, if necessary.

1. How are advertisements in business magazines different from advertisements in fashion, sports, and entertainment magazines? Compare and contrast.

2. Which magazines' advertisements give the reader the most information? How do they provide more information? Explain.

3. Why do you think more information is provided in advertisements in some types of magazines, and less information is provided in advertisements in other types of magazines? Explain.

Something for Everybody -

THERE ARE MORE THAN 19,000 different magazines in the United States. Most magazines contain both editorial and advertising content. (Editorial content is the articles or stories that are put in magazines by writers and editors.) In 2006, the ratio for consumer magazines was 47 percent advertising, 53 percent editorial content. This means there are millions of pages of magazine advertisements each year.

While newspaper circulation is declining in the United States, magazine circulation is increasing. However, rather than having fewer magazines with larger circulations, we continue to see more magazines with smaller circulation figures. This is because very few magazines today are directed at the general population. Instead, magazines focus on particular **demographic** and **psychographic** groups. For instance, women's fashion magazines are aimed at different age groups; *Vogue* is intended for readers who are older than the average reader of *Seventeen*. Some women's fashion magazines are aimed at women who are members of minority groups. Many magazines are directed at people with specific interests or hobbies. For example, there are dozens of music magazines focused on different styles of music, or focused on different types of musical instruments. There are magazines aimed at dog owners, at cat owners, and so on. The intention behind this specialization is to deliver a particular type of reader to the advertiser.

Go into a library, a bookstore, or any other store that carries a large number of magazines. Flip through three magazines that you've never read before. Consider the questions on the next page. Write your response in the chart provided. Use another sheet of paper, if necessary.

Activity 3: Something for Everybody *(continued)*

1. List the three magazines. Write down what type of reader you think that each type of magazine is directed toward. Include demographic and psychographic information for each. What clues helped you to determine the target audience?

Magazine	Target audience/reader	Clues

2. What was more helpful when you were trying to determine the type of reader of each magazine—the editorial content or the advertising? Explain.

Bad Billboards—A Bad Influence?- - - - - - - - - - - - - - -

A SURVEY IN ST. LOUIS, MISSOURI, found twice as many billboards in black neighborhoods as in white neighborhoods. Almost 60 percent of the billboards in the black neighborhoods advertised alcoholic beverages and cigarettes. In another study in Philadelphia, 60 of the 73 billboards in a 19-block area were found to advertise cigarettes or alcohol. In Baltimore, a study found that most of the billboards in that city were in poor black neighborhoods, and that most of the billboards in those neighborhoods advertised alcohol or tobacco products. (Tobacco companies agreed to stop advertising on billboards in April 1999.)[1]

A few people have taken it upon themselves to paint over billboards in their neighborhoods that advertise alcoholic beverages. The claim by those who paint over the billboards is that companies are preying upon poorer neighborhoods, because alcoholic beverages create health risks.

Consider the following questions. Write your response in the space provided. Use another sheet of paper, if necessary.

1. Do you agree or disagree with people who want to keep billboards for alcoholic beverages out of some neighborhoods? Explain.

Some people believe that companies that sell alcohol and tobacco products should be very careful about how they advertise. These people also believe that if the companies are not careful enough, then the government should be able to regulate what alcohol and tobacco companies can or cannot say in their advertisements.

Other people believe that alcohol and tobacco companies should be able to do what they want and let people make up their own minds about whether or not to buy alcohol or tobacco.

2. Which side do you believe makes the best argument? Explain.

[1]Statistics were gathered by Vernellia R. Randall, Professor of Law at the University of Dayton

Bad Billboards Everywhere? -

THE WORD *AESTHETICS* means a concern for beauty. Some people believe that billboards, which are usually along roadways, hurt the aesthetics of many roadways that pass through areas of natural beauty, such as countrysides and seasides. Even in cities, these people argue, the billboards only make a less-than-beautiful situation worse. People who are opposed to billboards also claim that the billboards create traffic safety hazards. After all, most billboards are along roadways and are designed to get people's attention. This means distracting drivers, causing unsafe driving conditions.

Those who defend billboards (including advertisers and companies that own billboards) point to the First Amendment of the U.S. Constitution, which guarantees freedom of speech. Those who oppose billboards remind us that freedom of speech has never been interpreted as the freedom to say anything that anybody wants to say. For example, as U.S. Supreme Court Justice Oliver Wendell Holmes, Jr., once said, freedom of speech does not give us the right to yell "Fire!" in a crowded movie theater when there is not a fire, since that could create a dangerous situation in which panicky people could be trampled to death.

People who defend billboards also argue that because billboards help create more business for advertisers, billboards help the economy. The economic benefits include providing jobs for not only the billboard companies' employees, but also for the employees of the companies that advertise on billboards. Defenders of billboards also point out that the land on which billboards are placed is usually owned by someone other than the billboard company. Defenders of billboards argue that these landowners are legally entitled to use their property in a reasonable manner, including earning income from renting space to the billboard companies.

Consider the following questions. Write your response in the space provided. Use another sheet of paper, if necessary.

1. List the arguments given in favor of prohibiting billboards.

2. List the arguments given in favor of protecting billboards.

3. Which of these two positions do you support? Explain.

Several U.S. Supreme Court cases have said that commercial speech (which includes advertising) is not protected by the First Amendment to the same degree that personal speech is. For example, if you want to encourage other people to vote for somebody you like, or if you want to encourage people to go to a particular church or temple, this type of speech is highly protected and very hard for the government to interfere with. If, however, you own a business and you want to encourage people to buy things from you, this type of speech is viewed by the courts as less important, so it is not as protected. This means the government may be able to place restrictions on advertising by businesses, though the government may not similarly restrict a person's political or religious speech (grouped together under the term *ideological speech*).

4. Do you agree with the U.S. Supreme Court—that commercial speech is not as important as ideological speech? Explain.

Newspapers versus Magazines: You Decide - - - - - - -

ABOUT ONE-HALF TO TWO-THIRDS of American adults read newspapers each day. It has been found that the older a person is, the more likely she or he is to read a newspaper each day. About 72 percent of people age 65 and older read a newspaper each day, while about 40 percent of people between the ages of 18 and 24 read a newspaper each day. It has also been found that the more educated a person is, the more likely she or he is to read a newspaper. Similarly, the more money a person makes, the more likely she or he is to read a newspaper. In general, though, most daily newspapers are directed at just about everybody in that newspaper's community who can read. Many newspaper advertisements are for local advertisers, but newspapers also contain advertisements for national companies.

Pretend you work for a chewing gum company that sells its chewing gum products throughout the United States. You must decide if you should advertise in local newspapers or national magazines. Newspaper advertisements are usually less expensive than magazine advertisements. This means that if you choose to run your advertisements in newspapers, you will be able to advertise in more newspapers than magazines. If you choose to advertise in local newspapers, you will advertise in the 100 largest cities in the country. If you advertise in magazines, you will choose from 20 of the 100 most popular national magazines. (Do not worry about which magazine titles you will choose.)

In making your decision, consider the following:

- Do you want to use color in your advertising? (Color is common in most magazines and rare for advertising in most newspapers.)

- Who will see your advertisements in newspapers?

- Who will see your advertisements in magazines?

- Do you want to advertise in 100 newspapers that are read by various types of people, or do you want to advertise in 20 magazines that you will select based on a targeted audience of people who read those magazines?

Consider the following questions. Write your response in the space provided. Use another sheet of paper, if necessary.

1. List three advantages of advertising the gum in newspapers instead of in magazines. Explain.

2. List three disadvantages of advertising the gum in newspapers instead of in magazines. Explain.

3. List three advantages of advertising the gum in magazines instead of in newspapers. Explain.

4. List three disadvantages of advertising the gum in magazines instead of in newspapers. Explain.

5. List three facts that you would want to know about the demographics of chewing gum consumers before making a decision about advertising in a newspaper or in a magazine. Explain why you would need each piece of information.

The objectives of this unit are to help students:

- understand the commercial nature of emerging media

- scrutinize the motives and techniques of firms that engage in stealth marketing

- analyze the tension between interstate commerce and individual privacy

- rely on their own creativity and imagination in generating new ideas for the new media

THE INTERACTIVITY OF THE INTERNET and other new media offers potential benefits to both advertisers and consumers. Interactivity allows advertisers to tailor their messages to individual Web users, and to gather often-instantaneous feedback about what types of advertising do and do not work. Consumers can benefit from two-way communication with advertisers, but significant privacy issues also arise. Students tend to have much less concern for privacy than do older adults. Part of this may simply be a generational difference in an American society that is increasingly information driven. Senior citizens generally have a greater concern for privacy than do middle-aged adults, who usually have greater concerns about privacy than teenagers do. Students often are flattered that advertisers want to know what they think. The challenge for the teacher in this unit is to have the students understand the consequences of providing information about themselves to advertisers.

In This Unit

Portal: The Fancy Word for a Start Page explains the advertising functions of start pages on the Internet.

gURL.com: It Says It's for Girls. Is It by Girls? has students investigate a commercial Web site that aggressively collects information about consumers while using stealth marketing techniques.

A Portal for Teenagers, by Teenagers may be best undertaken as a group project. This activity allows students to be creative as they undertake the design of their own start page for teenagers.

And They're Just Getting Started! requires students to count the number of advertisements they encounter in a typical surfing session.

E-Commerce has students evaluate the effectiveness of Internet marketing and provides students with the opportunity to develop some marketing ideas of their own.

4YEO (For Your Eyes Only) allows students to investigate the interactivity of text messaging.

Custom Advertisements asks students to explore how advertisers use consumers' personal information and interests to generate customized advertising.

TEENAGERS ARE ONE OF THE MOST attractive consumer age groups to advertisers. Teenagers are also one of the most difficult groups to reach. Teenagers watch less television and read newspapers less often than do older people. Teenagers spend less time at home, as they use mobile communications away from home. This unit focuses on how advertisers are beginning to move away from older forms of advertising media such as television, radio, and print, and are turning to what we will call "new media."

These new media include Web sites such as MySpace, Facebook, and other social networking sites; video games and virtual worlds; and text-enabled cell phones. In the near future, teenagers are also expected to embrace electronic forms of newspapers and magazines. These new electronic publications are available not just on computers, but also on cell phones and other wireless devices.

The interactive nature of many new forms of information and entertainment media, as well as the ability to mass-customize these media, will allow advertisers to pinpoint their teenage audiences more effectively. Advertisers will be better able to measure whether their advertisements get you to try their product or service. This is because they will know if you actually click on their on-screen advertisements or respond to a text message sent to you. In virtual worlds, such as *Second Life*, advertisers are using avatars that interact with teenagers and others who visit those virtual worlds.

The word *internet* was first used in 1982. But the history of the Internet actually begins in the 1960s, as organizations involved in national defense began to design new ways of connecting their computers so that they could "talk" to one another. In 1991, the World Wide Web was introduced. Mosaic, the first graphics-based Web browser, followed in 1993. Mosaic was important because it allowed us to see pictures and photographs instead of just words. Before Mosaic, most Internet communication was text-based only.

Online advertising first became a widespread practice around 1996. Perhaps the reason that commercial advertisers became most excited about the Internet is that it allows interactivity. This means that instead of advertising being a "one-way street" with the information coming only from the advertiser, the Internet allows advertisers to receive communications from consumers. So, interactivity allows advertisers to quickly find out which advertising messages work and which ones do not.

Interactivity also allows advertisers to build a database about consumers, which allows advertisers to conduct **data mining.** For example, if a teenager subscribes to a magazine, the magazine (and its advertisers) may know nothing about that subscriber except his or her name and address. Inside the magazine, the magazine might feature a contest or an opinion poll that asks the reader to go to the magazine's Web site. Once there, the magazine can ask for **demographic** and **psychographic** information about the reader: his or her age, hobbies, likes and dislikes, and so forth. Or an advertisement inside the magazine might include the advertiser's Web site and encourage readers to go to that site. That advertiser's Web site might ask for similar demographic and psychographic information.

Another, somewhat controversial way that Internet sites learn about you is by use of **cookies.** Cookies are unique identifiers put on your computer by Web sites when you surf the Internet. Some cookies are actually quite helpful to you, the computer user. For example, if you have a personal start page on your computer, such as My Yahoo, the cookie tells Yahoo who you are each time you log on and presents the information that you've asked for, such as your personal horoscope, your favorite sports teams' scores, the weather in your community, and so on. Also, when you shop at Web sites that you commonly visit, the cookie keeps information about your shipping address and credit card number, among other things. Sometimes, however, cookies are used to "spy" on you. It has been found that many Web surfers freely reveal information about themselves without concern about their privacy.

Advertisers also use cookies to conduct **behavioral targeting.** This process allows online advertisers to identify which types of Web sites a viewer visits to determine the types of products or services that the viewer might be interested in buying. Advertisers use this information to place appropriate advertisements on the Web sites that a particular viewer visits. For example, suppose that you visited the Web sites for three different colleges, all of them in Florida, and then you visit MySpace. You might see an advertisement for another Florida college at the MySpace site, based on your recent Internet usage.

Less sophisticated and more common is **contextual targeting.** This process doesn't record a viewer's previous Internet usage, but focuses instead on one Web page at a time. For example, if a viewer goes to a Web site that discusses a certain musical group, an advertisement for that musical group or similar groups may appear on that page. Of course, if advertisers know that fans of that musical group also like a particular type of candy, that Web page may include an ad for that type of candy.

In 1998, the U.S. government's Federal Trade Commission enacted the Children's Online Privacy Protection Rule, under the direction of Congress. This rule applies to operators of commercial Web sites and online services directed to children under the age of 13, and to general-audience Web sites and online services that knowingly collect personal information from children under 13. Among other things, the rule requires that Web sites get consent from a parent or guardian before collecting personal information from children.

Some consumers enjoy the interactivity that cookies provide—they feel that it allows advertisers to customize information to consumers' personal attitudes and habits. Others feel that interactivity is intrusive. They believe that the Internet allows advertisers to intrude in our lives, and perhaps violate our privacy.

Advertising on the Internet takes two basic forms: advertising banners and Web sites maintained by an advertiser. For example, let's say you are reading a news story at a **portal** such as MSN.com. The MSN

Ad Buzz *(continued)*

site may have a banner advertisement for Abercrombie & Fitch—even though you were not looking for information about clothing, you have now seen the advertisement. Oftentimes, a banner advertisement is a **click-through.** This means that if you click on the banner advertisement, you will be led to Abercrombie & Fitch's own Web site. This Web site is advertised in Abercrombie & Fitch's magazine advertisements and in promotional displays in its stores. The Web site allows you to do online shopping. It also includes music downloads, photographs of models, e-mail postcards that you can send to friends, and other items. If lots of visitors to the site click on one type of postcard, but not another, the company learns what sorts of pictures are popular with its consumers and what are not. This is the value of interactivity to the company—it now knows what types of pictures to use in its advertising and what to avoid.

Cell phone providers know a lot about you. They know your name and where you live, and they have access to either your financial records or those of the adult who helped you get your cell phone. Advertisers who use text messages or other ways to advertise to you on your cell phone use this information to customize the types of products or services they offer to you and the types of messages they send you.

Remember that television and radio were created as commercial media from the beginning. The entertainment and information that television and radio often provide us for free is actually paid for by advertisers. Similarly, the content provided on new media costs money to those who make that information and entertainment available to us. Many of those who create new media hope to make money through advertising.

Portal: The Fancy Word for a Start Page - - - - - - - - -

MANY INTERNET USERS have established start pages (also called home pages) where they begin their Internet surfing. Examples include iGoogle, My Yahoo, My Excite, and My MSN. These sites are attractive to users because they allow users to collect information that is important or interesting to them, such as local news and weather, television listings for favorite channels, information about favorite entertainers and sports teams, even personal daily horoscopes. The companies that provide these customizable start pages also gather information from cookies to present advertisements from companies that are seeking demographic and psychographic profiles. For example, a start page for a 42-year-old person might have advertisements for weight loss programs (especially in early January, when lots of middle-aged people make New Years' resolutions to lose weight). A banner advertising the latest lipstick colors might appear on the start page of a teenage female, while a banner advertising a basketball event might appear on the start page of a teenage male.

The companies that provide free start pages to Web surfers make a profit from this service by charging the advertisers who place banners or other advertisements on those start pages. This is similar to radio or broadcast television—the user does not pay for the medium, the advertiser does. However, unlike radio or television, advertisers on start pages can directly measure response to their advertisements. This occurs when we click on a banner; something that very few (less than 1 percent) of us do.

Consider the following questions. Write your response in the space provided. Use another sheet of paper, if necessary.

1. What do you think a Web portal (such as Google or Yahoo) does with the information it learns about you when you create a personal home page or start page, when you buy things at a sponsored site, or when you send e-mail through the portal's e-mail server (such as Gmail or Hotmail)? List everything you think that portal might do with that information. Explain your thinking.

Now, go to any portal (yahoo.com, google.com, msn.com, etc.), scroll to the bottom of the page, and click on "Privacy Policy." Read through the policy.

2. Summarize the privacy policy.

3. After reviewing this privacy policy, do you feel comfortable that the site is protecting your privacy? Explain.

gURL.com: It Says It's for Girls. Is It *by* Girls? - - - - - -

JWT (FORMERLY J. WALTER THOMPSON) is the largest advertising agency in the United States. Bob Jeffrey, the chief executive of JWT, said, "(Advertisers) need to stop interrupting what people are interested in and be what people are interested in." **Stealth marketing** occurs when an advertiser tries to make it look as though it is not engaging in marketing activities when it actually is. *Stealth* means "secret." Since many consumers grow tired of advertising, and since there is so much advertising that society often seems cluttered with it, advertisers often search for methods of advertising that is secretive or sneaky.

Visit gURL.com. Spend some time clicking around the site. Consider the following questions. Write your response in the space provided. Use another sheet of paper, if necessary.

1. List the different ways this Web site tries to gather information about its visitors.

2. Use the chart below to record the different types of information this Web site tries to gather. Explain why you think the Web site wants this information. If you think the Web site does not really want a particular piece of information (it's just acting as if it cares), explain your thinking.

Type of information gathered	Why gathered?

Unit 7: Advertising and the New Media

Activity 2: gURL.com: It Says It's for Girls. Is It *by* Girls? *(continued)*

3. Research on the Web. Find out who owns gURL.com. What else does that company own?

4. How is gURL.com an example of stealth marketing? Explain.

Activity 5: E-Commerce (continued)

Find online advertisements for three products. Describe how these ads tried to persuade you to click on them. Explain whether you thought the advertisements' persuasive techniques were effective or ineffective.

Product	What makes the ad clickable	Explain effectiveness

Imagine that you are working for an advertising firm that designs Internet advertisements companies that want to use the Internet to sell products or services.

List three things you would do to encourage Internet surfers to click on your advertisements. Explain why you think your ideas would work.

Encouragement	Why this would work

A Portal for Teenagers, by Teenagers - - - - - - - - - - - -

DESIGN YOUR OWN START PAGE for teenagers. Use another sheet of paper to design the page. Alternatively, use a software program to create the page. Try to make this site interesting to both males and females.

Consider working on the design as a group project. Ideally, males and females should work together in a group.

Before you begin, decide on what sort of information teenagers are interested in that would make them want to begin a surfing session at your Web site. Think about news, weather, sports, music, movies, fashion, and other types of information. Check existing portals such as Yahoo, Excite, and MSN. Make your site original.

Once your design is finished, consider the following questions. Write your response in the space provided. Use another sheet of paper, if necessary.

1. List each item on your Web site. Explain why you decided to include that information there.

2. Space on the Internet is not free. Somebody has to pay the bills. What types of advertisers do you think would be interested in paying to advertise on your Web site? Explain.

And They're Just Getting Started! - - - - - - - - - - - - -

AS MENTIONED IN THE AD BUZZ, the Internet became a commercial medium around 1996. In the years since, commercial Web sites and online advertisers have rapidly multiplied. Go online. Do what you normally do when you surf. As you're online, count the number of advertisements you encounter. Some advertisements will appear as banners, some will appear only as links, and some may appear as "pop-ups" (these are advertisements that pop up on your screen even when you do not click on an advertising link or banner). Count every single advertisement.

Consider the following questions. Write your response in the space provided. Use another sheet of paper, if necessary.

1. How many advertisements did you count?

2. Does that number surprise you? Explain.

3. How often do you click on banners or advertisers' links? Explain.

4. Does it bother you that there is so much advertising on the Internet? Why or why not? Explain.

E-Commerce - - - - - - - - - - - - - - - - - - -

THERE ARE MANY WAYS to make money on the Internet. Thous companies sell things to consumers directly, such as Amazon. So marketplace for other sellers, such as eBay. Other companies ma advertising on their sites. It costs you nothing to create a page on sites. The companies that own these sites make money by selling A magazine sets the price of its advertising based in part on how magazine. Television stations set the price of advertising based on a particular program. Web sites that sell advertising track how mc site each day, and many Web sites have thousands and thousand

It is one thing to see an advertisement, and quite another thing is selling. It is hard for an advertiser to know if a particular ad can magazine is successful in helping to sell products. An advertiser co advertisement on a Web site is doing its job. This is because many Internet are **click-throughs.**

In a click-through advertisement, the computer user must click on more information. In some cases, the user can make an online purc being advertised. Click-throughs have a pretty low response rate. Le click-through advertisements are actually clicked on. A 2-percent cli considered very successful.

This is a problem for the companies selling advertising on the Inte can quickly find out whether or not their advertisements are helping This is because they can calculate each day how many viewers actu advertisements. As a result, many advertisers who were excited abou years ago and were willing to spend millions of dollars on Internet a decided to spend much less, or have quit advertising on the Internet companies that hoped to make lots of money selling Internet advertisi business.

Surf around the Web, looking at the types of advertising that are c the Internet. Check out some of your favorite Web sites. Visit MySpace such as MSN, Excite, Yahoo, and CNN.

Fill in the charts on the next page. Write your response in the space another sheet of paper, if necessary.

1.

Im
for c

2

© 2009 Walch Education

112

Media Literacy: Advertising

© 2009 Walch Education

113

© 2009 V

4YEO (For Your Eyes Only) -------------------

MORE THAN 15 MILLION AMERICANS between the ages of 13 and 17 are cell phone subscribers, up from less than 12 million in 2004. That's a lot of kids who are talking and texting each other! There are many good reasons for young people to have a cell phone. There are also many advertisers who want to use text messages to reach those young people.

Callers make this easy for advertisers. Suppose someone sends a text message to order a pizza, to get sports scores from a television network, or to vote for a favorite contestant on a television show. Each time a person sends a text message, advertisers are gathering information about the cell phone owner's interests and habits. Today, cell phone service providers such as Verizon and AT&T receive about 20 percent of their income from delivering text messages to cell phone users.

Consider the following questions. Write your response in the space provided. Use another sheet of paper, if necessary.

1. Imagine that you are going to watch a sporting event on television. What types of advertisers do you think would want to text you before the game or sometime during the game? List at least three. Explain.

2. Imagine that you are driving or walking around town. Thanks to the Global Positioning System (GPS) technology in your phone, advertisers know where you are. What types of advertisers do you think would want to text you when you are driving or walking in a particular part of town? List at least three. Explain.

3. Imagine that it's 10 P.M. on a Friday or Saturday night. What types of advertisers do you think would want to text you at that time? List at least three. Explain.

4. Imagine that it's 8 A.M. on a Monday morning. What types of advertisers do you think would want to text you at that time? List at least three. Explain.

5. Imagine that you're getting ready to graduate from high school. What types of advertisers do you think would want to text you? List at least three. Explain.

Custom Advertisements -

As MENTIONED IN THE AD BUZZ for this unit, the interactivity of new media allows advertisers to pinpoint their customers. The more information consumers share about themselves online, the more advertisers know about buyers. This means that they know a person's likes and dislikes. Love rap music? Advertisers will place advertisements for rap artists on your portal page or your social networking page.

Take a moment and think about your likes and dislikes: what you like to eat, what you like to wear, what you like to watch, what you like to listen to. Also, think about what you like to do with your free time, which famous people you like or dislike, and how you like to spend your money.

Now imagine that an advertiser wants to get your attention so that the advertiser can try to sell you something.

Consider the following questions. Write your response in the space provided. Use another sheet of paper, if necessary.

1. Which advertisers do you think would most want to advertise to you? (Name either types of products or specific brands.) List at least three and explain why.

2. Do you think that these same advertisers who want to sell something to you now will want to advertise to you 10 years from now? Explain.

3. What Web sites should advertisers place ads on to get your attention? Explain.

4. How would you feel if an ad was personalized with your name or birthday? Would you be flattered, would it bother you, or would you not really care? Explain.

5. Which types of advertisers do you think would be most interested in knowing when your birthday is? Explain.

6. What other words, ideas, and designs do you think would be effective if an advertiser wanted to create a custom advertisement designed to attract you personally?

Glossary

behavioral targeting—the process that online advertisers use to identify which types of Web sites a viewer visits to determine the types of products or services that the viewer might be interested in buying. Advertisers use this information to place appropriate advertisements on the Web sites that a particular viewer visits. For example, a viewer who looks at a Web site for a florist service and later at a Web site for a candy company may see advertisements for other gift items, such as jewelry. This process makes use of a *cookie* (see below).

click-through—an advertisement on the Internet that, if clicked on, takes the viewer to a Web site at which the viewer can get more information about the product or make an online purchase of that product

contextual targeting—the process by which online advertisers use the information on a particular Web site an Internet user visits to place an appropriate advertisement. For example, if a viewer goes to a Web site that discusses a certain musical group, an advertisement for that musical group or similar groups may appear on that page.

cookie—a unique identifier put on your computer by a Web site when you surf the Internet. That cookie identifies you to the Web site when you return to it, or to other Web sites that share cookies with one another.

cool hunting—the process used by some advertisers to try to figure out what teens are interested in and what they are not interested in. Cool hunters interview teens online, at shopping malls, on the street, and near schools and social events. They use the information they find to develop advertising campaigns aimed at teens.

data mining—the practice by advertisers in which they use *demographics* and *psychographics* gathered about consumers to make advertising decisions (see below)

demographics—statistics about people grouped by such information as age, gender, ethnicity, geography, and income. For example, we know that the demographic group that watches the most television is women older than 60.

experiential marketing—an effort in recent years by advertisers to focus on the experience that consumers have with a product rather than the product itself. For example, advertisements for men's shaving products emphasize that the products help a man feel "more like a man." Similarly, an advertisement for a woman's perfume would emphasize femininity rather than how the product smells.

frequency—the number of times a particular group of people are exposed to an advertisement or a series of advertisements for a particular advertiser. Logically, it will cost the advertiser more to run advertisements more frequently.

hard cut—a film or video editing technique in which one scene or image on the screen abruptly ends and another scene or image abruptly appears. Hard cuts are increasingly common in television advertisements today, which may contain dozens of cuts in a 30-second advertisement. This constantly shifting visual imagery is used to attract and maintain the viewer's attention.

hierarchy—a method of ranking things by degree of importance (see ***Maslow's Hierarchy of Needs***)

jingle—a short song written particularly for the purpose of advertising a product on radio and television. The song will usually include the name of the product and may also have a short, catchy description of the product or its qualities. Famous examples include Burger King's "Have It Your Way" and Coke's "It's the Real Thing."

logo—the symbol that is used to identify a particular brand—for example, McDonald's golden arches; the red, white, and blue ball of Pepsi; and the Nike swoosh. The logo can also contain a word or words, such as the distinctive way in which the word *Coca-Cola* appears in Coke's logo.

machismo—a strong, sometimes exaggerated masculinity

Maslow's Hierarchy of Needs—categories of human needs, created by American psychologist Abraham Maslow. The categories are ranked in a pyramid from the most basic, such as food and water, at the bottom of the pyramid, to those that are not necessary for survival but that contribute to feelings of spiritual fulfillment at the top. The categories are:

physiological needs (food and water)

safety (physical and/or financial security)

social needs (need for love and acceptance)

esteem (respect of others, self-respect)

self-actualization (the need to fulfill oneself)

personification—the process in which one describes nonhuman objects in human terms

point-of-purchase advertising—this can include cardboard cutouts, banners, neon signs, and other types of advertising that are placed in stores, restaurants, and other places where the product being advertised is offered for sale

portal—a Web site that is often used by consumers as their start page. Such portals include Yahoo and MSN. Portals offer customizable content that is interesting to particular Web surfers, which helps those portals gather viewers. The portals then can make money by selling advertising space to advertisers who want to target surfers in particular demographics.

product placement—when advertisers pay producers of movies and television shows to have their products used by characters in those movies or television shows. The best-known example may be the placement of Reese's Pieces in the movie *E.T.* Product placement is a form of ***stealth marketing.***

pseudo-event—one form of stealth marketing. The prefix *pseudo* means "fake." Pseudo-events are fake news events that are really a form of advertising. Since the news media rely on advertising to make a profit, they often willingly participate in pseudo-events. A well-known example of a pseudo-event occurred when M&Ms candy added the color blue.

pseudonym—a fictitious name, especially a pen name

psychographics—statistics about people grouped by their interests, attitudes, values, and habits (including buying habits)

puffery—a claim by an advertiser that sounds good, but cannot be truly measured, evaluated, or compared—for example, an advertisement that tells you that a product is "the coolest thing ever"

push/pull marketing—marketing that refers to the customer's purchasing experience. In push marketing, advertisers "push" what they want to sell toward customers through a variety of methods. In pull marketing, customers "pull" information about what they want to buy toward themselves.

qualitative research—research by advertisers that focuses on what types of people are exposed to an advertisement, remember an advertisement, buy the advertised product, etc. The description of types of people and the qualities they share may be based on *demographics* or *psychographics.* Contrast with *quantitative research.*

quantitative research—research by advertisers that focuses on the quantity (number) of people who are exposed to an advertisement, remember an advertisement, buy the advertised product, etc. Contrast with *qualitative research.*

reach—the number of people who are exposed to an advertisement or a series of advertisements for a particular advertiser. Logically, it usually costs an increasing amount of money to reach a larger number of people.

recto—the right-hand page of a newspaper or magazine. English readers usually move their eyes automatically to the right-hand page, so an advertisement on a recto page will usually cost the advertiser more than an advertisement on the opposite *verso* (left) side.

self-actualization—the need to fulfill oneself, to become all that one is capable of being

stealth marketing—occurs when an advertiser is engaging in marketing activities but attempts to make it look as if it is not. *Pseudo-events* and *product placement* are two examples of stealth marketing.

tagline—a slogan, often presented at the end of a television or radio advertisement, or at the bottom of a newspaper or magazine advertisement. Its purpose is to help make the product and the advertisement memorable to the consumer. Examples include KFC's "We Do Chicken Right" and Nike's "Just Do It."

verso—the left-hand page of a newspaper or magazine. English readers usually move their eyes automatically to the right-hand page, so an advertisement on a verso page will usually cost the advertiser less than an advertisement on the opposite *recto* (right) side.

Additional Resources

Publications

Acuff, Daniel, and Robert Reiher. *Kidnapped: How Irresponsible Marketers Are Stealing the Minds of Your Children.* Chicago: Dearborn, 2005.

Hobbes, Renee. *Reading the Media: Media Literacy in High School English.* New York: Teachers College Press, 2006.

Johnston, Carla B. *Screened Out: How the Media Control Us and What We Can Do About It.* Armonk, NY: M.E. Sharpe, 2000.

Kilbourne, Jean. *Can't Buy My Love: How Advertising Changes the Way We Think and Feel.* New York: Touchstone, 2000.

Macedo, Donaldo, and Shirley R. Steinberg. *Media Literacy: A Reader.* New York: Peter Lang, 2007.

Mierau, Christina B. *Accept No Substitutes: The History of American Advertising.* Minneapolis: Lerner, 2000.

Potter, W. James. *Media Literacy.* 4th ed. Thousand Oaks, CA: Sage, 2008.

Quart, Alissa. *Branded: The Buying and Selling of Teenagers.* New York: Basic Books, 2003.

Silverblatt, Art. *Media Literacy: Keys to Interpreting Media Messages.* Westport, CT: Praeger, 1995.

Silverblatt, Art, and Ellen M. Enright Eliceiri. *Dictionary of Media Literacy.* Westport, CT: Greenwood, 1997.

Sivulka, Juliann. *Soap, Sex, and Cigarettes: A Cultural History of American Advertising.* Belmont, CA: Wadsworth, 1997.

Web Sites

Adbusters: www.adbusters.org

National Association for Media Literacy Education: www.namle.net

Center for Media Literacy: www.medialit.org

Center for Social Media: www.centerforsocialmedia.org

Children Now: Media: www.childrennow.org/issues/media

Commercial Alert: www.commercialalert.org

Just Think: www.justthink.org

Media Awareness Network: www.media-awareness.ca

Media Education Foundation: www.mediaed.org

Media Literacy.com: www.medialiteracy.com

Media Literacy Online Project: www.interact.uoregon.edu/medialit/MLR/home

PBS Frontline: The Merchants of Cool: www.pbs.org/wgbh/pages/frontline/shows/cool

PBS Teachers Media Literacy: www.pbs.org/teachers/media_lit

Turner Learning: Propaganda: http://cgi.turnerlearning.com/cnn/coldwar/cw_prop.html

SmartGirl: www.smartgirl.org

WALCH EDUCATION®

extending and enhancing learning

Let's stay in touch!

Thank you for purchasing these Walch Education materials. Now, we'd like to support you in your role as an educator. **Register now** and we'll provide you with updates on related publications, online resources, and more. You can register online at www.walch.com/newsletter, or fill out this form and fax or mail it to us.

Name _____ Date _____

School name _____

School address_____

City _____ State _____ Zip _____

Phone number (home) _____ (school) _____

E-mail _____

Grade level(s) taught _____ Subject area(s) _____

Where did you purchase this publication? _____

When do you primarily purchase supplemental materials? _____

What moneys were used to purchase this publication?

    [   ] School supplemental budget

    [   ] Federal/state funding

    [   ] Personal

    [   ] Please sign me up for Walch Education's free quarterly e-newsletter, *Education Connection.*

    [   ] Please notify me regarding free *Teachable Moments* downloads.

    [   ] Yes, you may use my comments in upcoming communications.

COMMENTS _____

_____

_____

_____

Please FAX this completed form to 888-991-5755, or mail it to:

Customer Service, Walch Education, 40 Walch Drive, Portland, ME 04103